The Word Finder

The Word Finder

Albert and Joan Rowe

BASIL BLACKWELL

Books by Albert Rowe

Active Anthologies, Books 1-3
British Teaching and its Contribution to Secondary Education
Desk Book of Plain English
English for Living, Books 1—4
English Through Experience, Books 1—5 (with Peter Emmens)
Federico García Lorca: Lyrics and Shorter Poems (translation)
Federico García Lorca, the Man and his Poetry
Language Links
Language Skills
Let's Laugh: Topliner Book of Humour
People Like Us: Short Stories for Secondary Schools
Poems   Federico García Lorca (translation)
Pollen Girl: Rockets
Positive English, Books 1-4
St Ives Boy's Summer and Other Poems
The Education of the Average Child
The Harmonica and Recorder Teacher's Manual (with Gareth Walters)
The Quest of Julian Day (adapted)
The School as a Guidance Community
Twenty Poems of Love and a Song of Desperation by Pablo Neruda
  (translation)

© Albert Rowe 1983

First published 1983

Published by
Basil Blackwell Publisher
108 Cowley Rd
Oxford OX4 1JF

British Library Cataloguing in Publication Data

Rowe, Albert
  The Word Finder
  1. English language
  Juvenile literature
  I. Title   II. Rowe, Joan
  423'.1   PE1591

ISBN 0 631 13201 5   hardback   ISBN 0 631 91950 3   paperback

Typesetting in 10/11 Paladium by Getset (BTS) Ltd, Eynsham, Oxford
Printed in Great Britain

To the Student

This book has been written to help you to choose the word that expresses your meaning exactly rather than write the first word that comes into your head.

It consists of 804 numbered headwords printed in **bold** type, and more than 7,000 related words. The headwords are among the commonest words we use when we write. Below each are a number of related words from which we can choose the word we wish to use if we do not wish to use the headword itself.

The words below each headword are as follows:

1 Synonyms. These are not defined because they mean the same, or nearly the same, as the headword itself.

2 Alternatives. These are in italics. They are closely related to the headword. The meaning of each is carefully defined to help you to make up your mind which you would like to use.

3 Extensions. These are also in italics and widen your choice still further. Most you will know, but some you will need to look up in your dictionary.

The Index lists all the words in their alphabetical order. Use it to look up the word you are thinking of using, then study the headword section in which it appears to choose the word that will best express your meaning.

1 abandon v.

desert leave

discard put aside as unwanted
get rid of throw away
jettison throw goods overboard to
  lighten a ship in distress
leave go away from
relinquish give up, usually to give up
  possession

forsake surrender

2 ability n.

capability capacity

aptitude natural ability, especially in
  learning
cleverness quickness in learning, or
  skill in using hands or body
gift special aptitude
potential possibility for developing
  or being developed
power vigour, energy, strength
talent special or very great ability

endowment ingenuity mastery

3 abolish v.

annul cancel; declare invalid
nullify cause or declare to have no
  effect
repeal cancel, especially in law
retract take back a statement or offer
  made
revoke withdraw or cancel a decree
  or licence
supersede replace, especially as an
  improvement on

eradicate

4 about prep.

concerning regarding respecting

dealing with

5 about to prep.

prepared to ready to soon to

6 about adv. and prep.

approximately more or less roughly

approaching close to

7 above adv.

at the top high up on high
overhead

8 absolutely adv.

certainly completely fully totally
unconditionally utterly wholly

9 abuse v. (i)

misapply misuse

exploit use a person unfairly for one's
  own profit
impose on take unfair advantage of

take advantage of

10 abuse v. (ii)

rail against complain or protest
  about; reproach strongly
revile criticize angrily in abusive
  language

11 accept v.

get come into possession of
receive take in something sent or
  given
take get possession of

abide by agree to assent to
comply with take on

12 **acceptable** adj.

commendable worthy of praise
proper suitable, correct
respectable having character and
  standards suited to society
worthy deserving respect or support

adequate all right fitting

13 **accident** n.

misadventure mischance misfortune

disaster sudden or great misfortune

calamity catastrophe

14 **accidental** adj.

unintentional unplanned unpremeditated

chance unplanned; happening by
  luck or fate
haphazard happening in a disorderly
  manner
unforeseen unexpected

15 **accuse** v.

charge

allege state or declare without proof
censure express strong disapproval
impute attribute wrongdoing to
  someone

16 **across** prep.

confronting *facing* *fronting*
on the other side of *opposite to*
over

17 **across** adv.

astraddle *astride* *crosswise*
transversely

18 **act** n.

action deed

conduct behaviour
performance notable action; carrying
  out

enterprise exploit

19 **act** v.

assume take on or undertake
behave bear oneself in an acceptable
  way
feign put on a false air
pretend give a deceiving appearance

fake sham

20 **addicted** adj.

dedicated to working hard for a
  special purpose
dependent on unable to do without
devoted to loving or loyal to a
  particular activity or person
hooked obsessed by, usually drugs

21 **admire** v.

look up to think highly of

esteem respect greatly
honour show or feel great respect
respect think highly of
revere feel awe for
venerate honour as hallowed or
  sacred

22 **adult** adj.

full-grown *fully developed*
grown-up *mature*

23 **advise** v.

counsel

enjoin order or command

guide influence strongly
recommend offer as the best course
suggest propose for acceptance or
  rejection
urge beg or persuade strongly

prescribe

24 affair n.

*business episode happening pro-
ceedings transaction undertaking*

25 affect v. (i)

influence

change cause to become different
impress upon make the importance
  of something clear
modify make partial changes in
play on make use of a person's
  sympathy for one's own advantage
sway have influence over

26 affect v. (ii)

move stir touch

agitate cause anxiety to
hurt cause pain to a person's feelings
perturb make anxious or uneasy
soften make less able to resist
impress make an impression on; have
  a favourable effect on

inflict

27 afraid adj.

alarmed fearful frightened scared

apprehensive feeling anxious,
  especially about the future
cowardly unable to face danger,
  pain, or hardship
jittery feeling anxious before an event
nervous easily agitated
panic-stricken filled with uncontrollable fear

terrified filled with very great fear
timid easily alarmed; lacking courage

craven timorous

28 afterwards adv.

later subsequently then

29 again adv.
another time

afresh anew

30 agile adj.
nimble well-coordinated

spry active and brisk
supple bending easily

light-footed

31 agree v. (i)
consent

accept take willingly; take as true
admit accept as true or based on
  truth
allow agree that something is true or
  acceptable
approve feel that something is good
  or suitable
grant agree that something is true

concur reconcile

32 agree v. (ii)
correspond

be appropriate be suitable or proper
fit be right and proper; be well
  adapted
match equal in ability, skill, or
  appearance
resemble be like

suit   satisfy or please; be convenient for
tally   correspond; be similar

coincide   *conform*

33   aim   n.

goal   object   purpose

ambition   strong desire to achieve something
plan   considered arrangement for some future activity
resolution   something one intends to do; mental pledge

intention   *endeavour*

34   alert   adj.

wide-awake

attentive   taking careful notice; listening carefully
prepared   ready to do something
vigilant   continually watchful
watchful   careful to notice things

heedful   *prudent*

35   alive   adj.

active   energetic

bustling   full of noisy activity
dynamic   full of power and activity
spirited   displaying vigour
sprightly   gay and full of energy
vital   full of life and force

36   all   adj.

complete   *entire*   *total*

37   allow   v.

let   permit   give permission

approve of   agree officially to
authorize   give power to or permission for

grant   permit what is requested
put up with   suffer without complaining
tolerate   permit without protest or interference

38   almost   adv.

nearly

all but   *close to*   *just about*
not quite   *virtually*   *wellnigh*

39   also   adv. & conj.

as well

additionally   *in addition*
including   *plus*   *too*

40   although   conj.

even if   *even though*   *granting that*
in spite of the fact that   *though*

41   altogether   adv.

completely   *entirely*   *totally*
wholly

42   always   adv.

at all times   *constantly*   *endlessly*
eternally   *everlastingly*   *evermore*
every time   *for ever*
on every occasion   *perpetually*
unceasingly   *without end*

43   among   prep.

amid   *amongst*   *in the middle of*
in the thick of   *surrounded by*

44   amount   n.

sum   total

aggregate   a mass or total made up of small parts

lot   a great quantity
number   a symbol or word indicating
  how many
quantity   an amount or number

45   angle   n.

*approach   attitude   point of view
standpoint*

46   angry   adj.

irate

annoyed   slightly angry
enraged   very angry
frantic   wildly agitated by anxiety
frenzied   state of wild, uncontrolled
  feeling
infuriated   intensely angry
irritable   tending to get angry over
  small things
raging   violently angry
ranting   talking in a loud, excited, or
  hostile way
raving   talking in a nonsensical or
  mad way

*cross   incensed   indignant   mad
nettled   peeved   riled   vexed*

47   animal   n.

beast   brute   creature   mammal

48   annoying   adj.

bothersome   irritating   troublesome

harassing   very tiring through
  continual worry or bother
nagging   finding fault continually
tormenting   teasing or worrying
  excessively
vexatious   very irritating or worrying

infuriating   maddening   vexing

49   another   adj.

*a different   a distinct   a further
an additional   an extra   a separate
a supplementary*

50   answer   v. (i)

reply   respond

acknowledge   report that one has
  received something
confirm   establish more firmly the
  truth of; say again to make
  more definite
rejoin   reply
retort   reply quickly, sometimes
  cuttingly, often wittily
riposte   reply quickly and cleverly

get back at   retaliate

51   answer   v. (ii)

solve

justify   give or be a good reason for
satisfy   provide with sufficient proof
  to convince

52   anyhow   adv. (i)

anyway   by any means   at all events
at any rate   in any case

53   anyhow   adv. (ii)

*carelessly   haphazardly   heedlessly
mindlessly   negligently   sloppily*

54   appear   v. (i)

emerge

come into view   come up or out
come to light   reveal by investigation
loom   appear close at hand or with
  threatening aspect
rise up   become visible

55 appear v. (ii)

look as if   look like   seem

strike one as being   wear the aspect of

56 approach v.

come close   come near   draw near
move closer to

57 argue v.

dispute

bandy words   exchange remarks in a
  quarrel
cavil   find fault unnecessarily
contend   compete; fight for something
debate   discuss or consider formally
quibble   make petty objections

58 around adv.

*far and wide   here and there
in all directions   in all parts
on all sides   on most sides*

59 artful adj.

crafty   cunning

canny   not easily deceived
foxy   not to be trusted
knowing   showing secret
  understanding
sly   dishonestly tricky

calculating   scheming   shifty

60 ashamed adj.

abashed   feeling ill at ease or confused
embarrassed   feeling awkward
humiliated   disgraced; having lost the
  respect of others

chagrined

61 ask v.

enquire

interrogate   question closely or
  formally
query   express doubts about
question   seek information
quiz   test or examine the knowledge
  of

beg   beseech   request

62 assess v.

judge

consider   think about
evaluate   calculate the value
investigate   examine thoroughly
review   re-examine or survey
weigh up   consider carefully

63 attack v.

assail   attack violently and
  persistently
assault   attack suddenly and violently
  with blows
beseige   surround with armed forces
blitz   attack suddenly and violently,
  especially from the air
bombard   send a barrage of shells
  against; bomb heavily
raid   make a sudden surprise visit to
  catch someone or seize something
storm   capture through using great
  violence, especially a fortress
strafe   spray with bullets from low-
  flying aircraft

64 attitude n.

demeanour   how a person behaves
  towards others
opinion   what one thinks on a
  particular point
outlook   a person's mental attitude or
  way of looking at something

*frame of mind   mental state
temperament*

65 attract v.

allure attract by offering something pleasant
charm please; win over; delight
enchant fill with intense delight

enamour

66 auburn adj.

bronze   copper   golden-brown
henna   reddish-brown
russet   rust

67 average adj.

ordinary   typical

middling neither good nor bad
moderate medium in amount, intensity, or rate
normal conforming to what is standard
standard generally recognized as correct

fair-to-middling   run-of-the-mill

68 aware adj.

conscious knowing; understanding
mindful giving thought or careful attention to; not forgetful of

alive to   conversant   informed
observant

69 awful adj. (i)

dreaded   dreadful   spine-chilling
terrible

70 awful adj. (ii)

distasteful   nasty   repulsive   shoddy
third-rate

71 awkward adj. (i)

cumbersome clumsy to wear or carry or manage
ill-adapted altered clumsily and unsuitably
unmanageable unable to be controlled
unsuitable not fitted for its purpose
unwieldy difficult to move, use, or control

inappropriate   inconvenient
inopportune   untimely

72 awkward adj. (ii)

clumsy

aggressive   crude   gawky   ungainly

73 baby n.

infant   newborn

foundling a deserted child of unknown parents
toddler child who has recently learnt to walk
tot very small child

bairn   nursling

74 bad adj.

corrupt accepting bribes; morally depraved
dangerous liable to cause harm
dishonest untruthful and untrustworthy
evil very bad; harmful; sinful
immoral not considered good or right
unscrupulous not caring about honesty or fairness
wicked greatly offending against what is right

criminal   villainous

75 bag n.

*attaché case   briefcase   carpet bag
carrier   duffle bag   grip
handbag   haversack   holdall
kitbag   pouch   purse   rucksack
sack   satchel   suitcase*

76 baggy adj.

loose   puffy   shapeless   slack

77 banish v.

exile   send away

expel   force to leave school or country
ostracize   refuse to have social
  dealings with
outlaw   declare to have lost the
  protection given by law

78 bar v. (i)

bolt   fasten   lock   lock up   secure

79 bar v. (ii)

ban   forbid officially·
boycott   refuse to have anything to do
  with
impede   make difficult to act or go
  forward
prohibit   forbid

blacklist   exclude   hinder

80 bay n.

basin   deep part of a harbour; wide
  part of a canal
bight   long inward curve in a coast
cove   small, sheltered opening in the
  coastline
creek   narrow, long inlet of water
  from sea or lake into the land
estuary   mouth of large river into
  which sea enters at high tide

fiord   deep, narrow arm of sea
  between cliffs, especially in Norway
gulf   area of sea partly surrounded by
  land, larger than a bay
harbour   place of shelter for ships
inlet   strip of water extending into the
  land from sea or lake, or between
  islands
mouth   place where a river enters the
  sea

81 become v.

*change into   come to be   develop into
evolve into   grow into   mature into
pass into   ripen into   turn into*

82 bed n.

bunk   narrow bed fixed to the wall
cot   child's bed with high sides
cradle   small bed for a baby, usually
  on rockers
crib   baby's cot
hammock   hanging bed of canvas or
  rope network
palliasse   straw mattress
recliner   armchair whose back can be
  lowered for sleeping on

83 beer n.

ale   pale-coloured beer
bitter   beer strongly flavoured with
  hops
lager   light gassy beer
mild   beer not strongly flavoured
stout   strong, dark beer

84 before adv.

*earlier   formerly   in the past
previously*

85 begin v.

commence   start

embark   begin an undertaking
establish   set up on a permanent basis
found   start a company or
  organization
inaugurate   begin officially or
  formally; open with a ceremony
initiate   start a scheme working;
  introduce, especially with a ceremony
instigate   start something happening
  by one's own action
launch   send off; start a project
pioneer   take part in a course of
  action that leads the way for others
  to follow

set in motion

86 begrudge v.

be jealous of   feel or show resentment
envy   feel discontent at another's
  qualities or possessions
resent   feel angry or bitter at

87 belief n.

acceptance   willingness to agree to
assent   agreement with an idea
assurance   strong faith in one's own
  ability; trustworthy statement
certainty   freedom from doubt;
  established fact
confidence   firm trust
faith   complete trust in a person or
  thing
reliance   confidence felt about
  something
trust   firm belief in the honesty,
  worth, or power of someone or
  something

88 believe v.

acknowledge   admit; recognize the
  existence of

assert   state forcefully
assume   take as true without proof;
  suppose
conclude   arrive at a belief or opinion
  by reasoning
consider   think about, especially so as
  to make a decision
deduce   decide from general principles
maintain   assert as true
recognize   acknowledge formally as
  being genuine

postulate

89 belongings n.

effects   personal effects   possessions

article   particular thing or object
gear   set of things collected together
  for a particular purpose
goods   movable property; articles of
  trade
kit   clothing and personal equipment
  of a soldier, sailor, traveller,
  or sportsperson
luggage   cases and bags of a traveller
property   thing or things owned

equipment

90 bend v.

contort   twist severely out of shape
curve   bend round with no sharp
  angles
flex   move so as to stretch and loosen
twist   move in a winding course
meander   follow a winding course

coil   loop   zigzag

91 beside prep.

alongside   by   by the side of
close by   near to   next to
on the edge of   not relevant to

92 besides adv,

*furthermore   moreover
on top of everything else*

93 besides prep.

apart from   except for   in addition

94 betray v.
break faith with

give away   inform against

95 beware v.

*be alert   be careful   be wary
guard against   take heed   watch out*

96 beyond prep.

*across   further on   in excess of
on the farther side of
on the other side of   out of reach of*

97 big adj.
large

*colossal   elephantine   enormous
gargantuan   gigantic   huge
immense   vast*

98 billowy adj.

*heaving   rippling   rolling   surging
tossing   undulating*

99 bit n.
fragment   piece   scrap

morsel   small piece of food
portion   part or share of something
sliver   small, thin, sharp piece cut or
   torn off

mouthful

100 bitter adj. (i)

acid   sharp-tasting; sour-tasting
biting   smarting and unpleasant in the
   mouth
pungent   strong, sharp taste or smell

acrid   astringent

101 bitter adj. (ii)

distressing   causing suffering, sorrow,
   or pain
grievous   seriously harmful; severe
harrowing   causing pain and worry

102 bitter adj (iii)

acrimonious   sharpness of manner or
   temper
caustic   sarcastic

103 black adj.

coal-black   black as coal
ebony   like the hard, dark wood of a
   tropical tree
pitch-black   completely black, with
   no light at all
raven   glossy black

*besmirched   dingy   grimy   sooty
sullied*

104 blame v.
hold responsible

cast aspersions on   make accusations
   without proof
reproach   express disapproval, not
   angrily but sadly

point the finger at

105 blank adj. (i)

*bare   unadorned   undecorated
unmarked*

106 blank adj. (ii)

bewildered puzzled
confused mixed up in thoughts and feelings
expressionless showing nothing in face or voice
poker-faced not revealing thoughts or feelings

107 blatant adj.

arrant utter; out-and-out; downright
brazen shameless
flagrant open and shameless
flaunting displaying in an offensive way
glaring very obvious
obtrusive unpleasantly noticeable
offensive insulting; disgusting

108 bleak adj.

arid parched and desert-like
cheerless dreary and without comfort
desolate dismal and deserted by people
exhausted used up completely
uncultivable unable to grow crops
unproductive producing little of value

unsheltered *windswept*

109 blue adj. (i)

azure sky-blue
aquamarine pale blue to greenish-blue colour
lapis lazuli brilliant deep blue
sapphire transparent bright blue
turquoise sky blue or greenish-blue

110 blue adj (ii)

despondent downcast unhappy

doleful mournful and dreary in a self-pitying way

glum in low spirits, especially because of disappointment

depressed

111 boastful adj.

bragging

arrogant proud and self-important in a rude way
blustering talking aggressively, especially with empty threats
crowing loudly exulting or triumphing
overbearing bossy in manner or action
vaunting bragging; blowing one's own trumpet

112 boat n.

craft

canoe long, light narrow boat, pointed at both ends, moved by a paddle
coracle small wicker-basket boat, covered with watertight material
dinghy small open boat for rowing or sailing
dugout boat made by hollowing a tree trunk
galleon large 15th-17th century sailing ship, usually Spanish
galley ancient or medieval warship or trader propelled by oars and/or sails
houseboat barge-like boat fitted up as a dwelling
kayak small, light, covered canoe, first used by Eskimos
launch large motor boat
packet boat for carrying mail, and often people as well
pinnace small boat used by a ship
punt flat-bottomed river boat propelled by a long pole
skiff small light boat for rowing, sculling or sailing

sloop   single-masted sailing vessel, rigged fore-and-aft

tender   boat travelling to and from a larger one to convey stores or passengers

tug   small powerful boat for towing others

yacht   light sailing boat, used either for racing or pleasure cruises

113   **bog**   n.

mire

fen   low-lying marshy or flooded land

marsh   land that is all or partly soft and wet

morass   stretch of soft, wet ground, dangerous for walking

quagmire   soft, wet area of land that gives way under the feet

swamp   permanently waterlogged ground, usually overgrown

114   **bold**   adj.

daring   unafraid

plucky   brave and determined

115   **bonus**   n.

award   given officially as a payment or prize

dividend   share of profits paid to shareholders or winners

fringe benefit   added favours or services given with a job

gratuity   money given in recognition of services rendered; a tip

handout   something distributed free of charge

present   something given or received as a gift

reward

116   **book**   n.

album   book used for collections, e.g. photographs, stamps

anthology   collection of passages from literature, especially poems

classic   work of literature of lasting importance

diary   daily record of events or thoughts

dictionary   book that lists words in alphabetical order, with their meanings

encyclopaedia   book or set of books dealing with branches of knowledge, usually in alphabetical order

handbook   small book giving useful facts

journal   daily record of news, events, or business dealings

ledger   business account book

log   detailed record of a ship's voyage or an aircraft's flight

manual   book, especially of instructions or information

manuscript   author's work as written or typed

novel   book-length story about imaginary people

paperback   book bound in a flexible paper binding

publication   something printed and issued to the public

romance   imaginative story of love and adventure

textbook   book for studying a particular subject

thesaurus   dictionary of words arranged according to likenesses in their meaning

thriller   exciting story

tome   large, heavy book

tract   pamphlet on a moral or religious subject

treatise   written work dealing systematically with one subject

volume   one of a set of books of the same kind

117 boost v.

advance help the progress of
advertise make thing known
 publicly, especially to encourage
 people to buy
advocate speak in favour of
back support and encourage, often
 with money
facilitate ease the path of
further help the progress of
promote help forward
publicize bring to the attention of the
 public

recommend

118 boring adj.

humdrum without change; dull and
 commonplace
irksome causing vexation,
 annoyance, or boredom
monotonous lacking variety
repetitious containing things said or
 done many times
tedious tiresome because of its
 length, slowness or dullness
unvaried unchanging

tiresome

119 boundary n.

limit

border edge; dividing line between
 two countries
circumference distance round a circle
 or circular area
frontier line where two countries
 meet
perimeter outer edge of an area
periphery outside edge of an area;
 outer or surrounding region of area

bounds

120 box n.

bin large, rigid container with lid
cabinet piece of furniture with
 drawers and shelves
caddy small box or tin for holding tea
carton box made from cardboard for
 holding goods

casket small, usually ornamental,
 box for holding valuables
chest large, strong box for storing or
 shipping things
coffer large, strong box for holding
 money and valuables
container box, barrel, or bottle for
 holding something
crate packing-case made of wooden
 slats
locker small cupboard or
 compartment where things can be
 stowed safely
receptacle something for holding or
 containing what is put into it
safe box or cupboard with thick
 metal sides and lock, used to store
 valuables
strong-box strongly-made small chest
 for valuables
trunk large box with hinged lid for
 transporting or storing clothes

121 boy n.

lad

adolescent young person between
 about 13 and 16
child young person below the age of
 puberty
juvenile young person
minor person not yet reached the age
 at which he is fully responsible in law
 for his actions
stripling young man
teenager person aged between 13 and
 19
urchin mischievous or needy child
youngster young person; child or
 youth
youth person between childhood and
 maturity

122 brave adj.

courageous fearless valiant

dauntless not discouraged or afraid
gallant honourable and high spirited
heroic quite exceptionally brave
intrepid daring and without fear

chivalrous

123 break v.

chip cut or break a small piece from the surface or edge
crack break without dividing into separate parts
crash have or cause to have a sudden violent and noisy accident
crush press so as to break, injure, or wrinkle; squeeze tightly
fracture break or crack, especially of a bone
grind crush into grains or powder by pressing between hard surfaces
shatter break suddenly and violently into small pieces
smash break or become broken suddenly and noisily into pieces
snap suddenly break off
splinter break into needle-like pieces
split divide along a length, especially with force

124 breathe v.

exhale breathe out
gasp catch the breath suddenly and audibly
inhale breathe in deeply
pant breathe with short, quick breaths
puff breathe rapidly and with effort
wheeze make a noisy whistling sound when breathing

respire

125 bright adj. (i)

glossy shiny and smooth
glowing giving out light and heat without flame
incandescent giving a bright light when heated
luminous giving out light; glowing in the dark
radiant giving out rays of light
shiny rubbed until bright

126 bright adj. (ii)

animated full of life and excitement
cheerful in good spirits
gay light-hearted and full of fun
lively full of life

127 brilliant adj.

blinding too bright to see clearly
dazzling bright and confusing
scintillating twinkling very brightly
sparkling shining brightly in small flashes
vivid intense, bright and clear

128 bring v.

cause make happen
conduct guide or lead
escort accompany someone
lead show the way

129 brunette adj.

brown-haired

130 brutal adj.

callous without feelings; hardened
inhumane not showing normal qualities of kindness, pity, or sympathy

vicious   merciless

131 build v.

construct

erect   put up

132 bungle v.

botch spoil or repair badly by lack of skill or care
mismanage handle badly or wrongly

133 busy adj.

*absorbed active engaged
occupied working*

134 busybody n.

backbiter person who talks spitefully about others in their absence
eavesdropper person who listens secretly to a conversation
gossip person who talks casually about other people's lives
meddler person who interferes in other people's affairs
muckraker person who seeks and tells unpleasant stories about others
newsmonger someone who enjoys gossiping
slanderer someone who deliberately spreads false reports about others
snooper someone who pries into the private business of others
tale-bearer someone who nastily spreads unkind or false stories about others

135 but conj. and prep.

*except nevertheless on the contrary
on the other hand save yet*

136 calm adj. (i)

peaceful quiet still

placid having a calm appearance or nature
serene completely calm and peaceful
tranquil undisturbed; not agitated

becalmed undisturbed

137 calm adj. (ii)

collected composed

imperturbable unable to be worried or excited

serene unable to be troubled or agitated

*cool cool-headed even-tempered
self-controlled self-possessed*

138 car n.

automobile motorcar

convertible car with a roof that can be folded down or removed
coupé closed two-door car with a sloping back
hatchback car with a sloping back hinged at the top so that it can be opened
hearse vehicle for carrying the coffin at a funeral
jalopy battered old car
jeep small sturdy motor vehicle with four-wheel drive
limousine large luxurious car, usually with glass between driver and passengers
roadster open car, especially with two seats
saloon car with roof, closed sides, windows, and a separate boot
sports car open, low-built fast car
taxi car with its driver hired by the public

139 care n.

anxiety trouble worry

apprehension feeling of fear or anxiety about a possible danger or difficulty
concern serious care for or interest in
misgiving feeling of doubt or slight fear or mistrust
uneasiness mental or physical discomfort

grief sorrow

140 careful adj.

cautious very watchful
chary cautious; wary
concerned giving time or attention to
conscientious showing or done with
  serious attention
meticulous giving great attention to
  detail; very exact
painstaking taking great care
protective wanting to keep from
  harm or injury
wary looking out for possible danger
  or difficulty

fastidious *finicky* *hesitant*

141 careless adj.

inattentive negligent thoughtless

neglectful leaving undone; not giving
  due care to
remiss neglecting duty
unheeding deliberately not listening
  or paying attention
unorganized unplanned and
  disorderly

blasé *happy-go-lucky*

142 careworn adj.

bowed down *dispirited* *exhausted*
haggard

143 carry v.

bear

cart carry with great labour
convey take or carry from one place
  to another
deliver take to the intended person or
  place
drag pull along with effort or
  difficulty
haul pull or drag forcibly; transport
  by a truck
lug carry or drag with great effort

support hold in position; bear the
  weight of
transmit send or pass from one
  person, place, or thing to another
transport take from place to place

144 case n.

matter

affair concern or business
circumstance manner, time, place of
  an act or event; detail or fact
event thing that happens, especially
  of importance
instance example; particular case
situation place; position

plight *problem*

145 casual adj. (i)

fortuitous happening by a lucky
  chance
nonchalant casually unconcerned or
  not interested
offhand short and disrespectful in
  speech and manner
unexpected happening without being
  previously thought of

casual adj. (ii)

informal without ceremony

146 catch v.

capture

arrest seize someone by authority of
  the law
grab seize something or someone
  with a sudden rough movement
net catch in, or as if in, a net
snare catch in, or as if in, a noose

take into custody

147 catching adj.

contagious able to be spread by touch or closeness
infectious able to be spread by air or water

transferrable transmissible

148 cause n.

reason

agent person or thing that produces an effect, change, or result
creator one who brings something into existence
inducement encouragement to do something
inspiration something or someone that rouses the mind and feelings to special activity
motive reason for action
originator person who begins or causes the beginning of something
source person or thing that supplies information; starting point
stimulus something that causes activity

explanation

149 celebrate v.

acclaim salute with cheering and clapping
commemorate honour or keep alive the memory of
extol praise very highly
observe follow a custom, tradition, law, or holiday
pay homage carry out a ceremony to honour someone

150 celebrated adj.

famous renowned

eminent very well-known and admired; outstanding

prominent important and well-known
respected very well thought of

acclaimed venerable

151 chair n.

armchair chair with raised sides or arms
deckchair portable folding chair of canvas on wood or metal frame
easy chair big comfortable chair, usually with arms
rocking chair chair on curved supports that can be moved gently backwards and forwards
seat anything that can be sat on
settee seat for two or more, with back and usually arms, part of a three-piece suite
throne special chair used by a king, queen, or bishop on ceremonial occasions
wheelchair invalid's chair on wheels

152 change v.

alter

convert change from one substance, state, use, or purpose to another
interchange put each of two things into the other's place
modify make slight changes
replace find or provide a substitute for
transform change completely in appearance or nature

recast restyle

153 changeable adj.

variable

chequered marked by frequent changes of good and bad luck

fickle not constant or loyal in love or
  friendship
inconstant changeable and unfaithful
  in feeling
indecisive not firm or steady in
  purpose or action
unreliable not able to be trusted
unstable tending to change suddenly
  in feelings or behaviour

154 chaos n.

confusion disorder

bedlam scene of wild, noisy activity
rumpus loud and angry dispute
turmoil state of great confusion,
  excitement, and trouble
upheaval great change and
  movement
upset disturbance of normal course
  of events

155 character n.

ego favourable image of oneself
individuality qualities that make one
  person different from another
nature fundamental qualities of a
  person or thing

attribute idiosyncrasy trait

156 charming adj.

appealing able to arouse pleasurable
  feelings
attractive pleasing in appearance or
  effect
delightful highly pleasing
engaging occupying the pleased
  attention of
winning persuasive
winsome sweetly charming in
  manner and appearance

*alluring beguiling captivating
enchanting enticing entrancing
irresistible*

157 chase v.

pursue run after

hunt pursue for food or sport, or
  with hostility
run down chase and overtake animal
  or person
shadow follow and watch secretly
stalk follow or approach game
  stealthily and quietly
track find and follow marks left by a
  moving person, animal or thing
trail follow marks left by person or
  animal

158 cheap adj.

inexpensive low-priced

bargain very cheap
economical avoiding waste
reasonable fair; not expensive
reduced lowered in price

159 cheat v.

deceive trick

delude mislead or trick
fleece charge far too much, or
  defraud
rook swindle; charge far too high a
  price
swindle obtain by fraud

160 cheek n.

impudence insolence pertness

audacity bold and reckless
  impudence

161 cheer v. (i)

applaud clap

cheer v. (ii)

gladden comfort

162 cheerful adj.

cheery   in good spirits

amiable   feeling and inspiring
  friendliness; good-tempered
jovial   full of cheerful good humour
joyful   full of happiness
merry   laughingly cheerful
optimistic   believing things will turn
  out well
vivacious   high-spirited

light-hearted

163 cheering adj.

heartening

auspicious   giving signs of future
  success
stimulating   making more vigorous or
  active

comforting   encouraging   reassuring

164 cheerless adj.

dreary   gloomy

dingy   dirty and faded
dismal   causing gloom and depression
drab   monotonous; dull
murky   dark and unpleasant
sombre   full of shadows

abandoned   depressing   uninviting

165 chiefly adv.

especially   mainly   predominantly
principally

essentially   most importantly;
  necessarily
particularly   for one definite or
  particular point

above all   first and foremost

166 choke v.

asphyxiate   make or become unable
  to breathe
block   obstruct
clog   make or become filled with thick
  or sticky matter
obstruct   place something to prevent
  or hinder movement or progress
smother   die or kill through lack of air
stifle   feel, or cause to feel, unable to
  breathe
strangle   kill by squeezing neck;
  throttle
suffocate   kill, or be killed, by lack of
  oxygen

garrotte   throttle

167 choose v.

pick   select

adopt   take and use as one's own
cull   select from flock and kill,
  especially surplus animals
elect   choose by vote
opt for   show preference for
prefer   like better
single out   separate from others for
  special treatment or notice

favour

168 chronic adj.

*continual   deep-rooted   ingrained
long-standing   persistent*

169 civil adj.

mannerly   polite

agreeable   to one's liking
courteous   polite and considerate in
  manner
deferential   showing polite respect
formal   correct in manner and
  behaviour
respectful   feeling or showing
  consideration or admiration

170 class n.

category   division   group

branch   subdivision
set   group of naturally connected
  things

171 claw v.

gouge   scoop or force out
lacerate   injure by tearing jaggedly
rend   tear with violent force
rip   tear quickly and violently
tear   pull apart or into pieces by force

172 clean adj

spotless   unsoiled

laundered   washed and pressed
scoured   cleaned by hard rubbing
  with a rough material
uncorrupted   moral; free from
  dishonesty and wickedness
unstained   without being discoloured
  or darkened in any way
untainted   without trace of decay or
  infection

173 clear adj. (i)

transparent

limpid   clear, calm and peaceful
translucent   allowing some light to
  pass through

174 clear adj. (ii)

bright   cloudless   sunny

175 clever adj.

brainy   intelligent   sharp-witted

accomplished   able to do many things
brilliant   outstandingly clever
gifted   having great natural ability

ingenious   clever at inventing new
  things or methods
inventive   able to invent or think in
  new ways
precocious   showing unusually early
  development of mind or body
resourceful   able to get round
  difficulties
sharp   quick to see, hear, or notice
  things
skilful   able to do something well and
  easily
smart   good or quick in thinking or
  speaking
talented   having very great natural
  ability or aptitude

176 climb v.

ascend   scale

clamber   climb with some difficulty,
  using both feet and hands
mount   get up on
scramble up   move hastily and
  awkwardly up a rough, steep slope

creep up   trail up   twine up

177 close v.

shut

close off   put up a barrier
close up   shut up completely
seal   close securely to prevent entry
seal off   close tightly to prevent
  escape or entry

barricade   blockade

178 close adj.(i)

compact   closely or neatly packed
  together
dense   massed closely together
stuffy   lacking sufficient fresh air

airless

close adj.(ii)

secretive hiding one's intentions or
plans

179 clutter n.

hotch-potch things mixed up without
any order
huddle confused mass of people or
things
jumble muddle; confused collection
of things
litter odds and ends of rubbish left
lying about
lumber useless or unwanted articles
stored away
mess untidy collection of things

180 coat n.

anorak short coat with hood to keep
out wind, rain, and cold
duffle coat loose coat of heavy cloth,
fastened with toggles
greatcoat heavy overcoat, especially
military
jerkin sleeveless jacket
parka jacket with hood, with fur
inside
tunic close-fitting jacket worn as part
of a uniform
windcheater sports jacket of thin but
windproof material, fitting closely
at waist and cuffs

*blazer   jacket   mackintosh
overcoat   raincoat   sports jacket*

181 coax v.

persuade

beguile win the attention or interest
of; amuse
cajole persuade by flattery or
pleasing talk
entreat beg earnestly or emotionally
flatter praise too much or insincerely
in order to please someone

wheedle persuade by flattery or
endearments; get something out
of someone
wile lure, beguile, or entice

182 code n.

criterion standard of judgement
guideline principle by which to set
standards or determine actions
law rule supported by government
power that members of society must
follow
morals rules of behaviour based on
people's sense of what is right or just
principles high personal standards of
what is right and wrong
rules orders that guide actions or
describe events

183 cold adj.

bitter piercingly cold
chilly unpleasantly cold
freezing cold enough for water to
turn to ice
frigid intensely cold
glacial extremely cold, reminding one
of a glacier
icy as cold as ice
sharp keen and biting
sunless without sunshine

184 collect v.

accumulate   gather

amass gather in great amounts
assemble fit, put, or gather together
compile collect or arrange into a list
or book
garner collect and store up
glean gather scraps of information;
pick up grain left after harvesters
harvest gather a crop
muster gather together troops for
inspection or duty

flock together   store up   stow away

185 **colour** v.

brighten add fresh colour
daub coat or smear roughly
dye stain; make something a
  specified colour
paint apply colour, especially with
  brush
shade darken so as to give the effect
  of light and shadow
tincture add a slight trace of colour
tinge change the colour slightly
tint apply or give a slight colour to

186 **come** v.

approach come nearer
arrive come to destination
reach go as far as

move towards

187 **comfort** v.

console

reassure remove fear or doubt
relieve make something less
  unpleasant, hard, or monotonous
solace comfort or cheer in distress
support help with sympathy,
  practical advice, or money

encourage

188 **comfortable** adj.

*at ease   at rest   cosy   homelike
relaxed*

189 **compare** v.

contrast show clearly the differences
  between two things
correlate compare and connect
  systematically
differentiate recognize as different
examine look at closely to find out
  something

judge give a decision or opinion
  about
liken point out the resemblance of
  one thing to another
measure estimate by comparing with
  some standard

190 **complacent** adj.

pleased with oneself   self-contented
self-satisfied

smug far too self-satisfied

191 **concerning** prep.

about   regarding   relating to

*referring to   respecting
with reference to*

192 **condemn** v.

censure express strong criticism or
  disapproval
convict prove or declare a person to
  be guilty of a crime
denounce speak publicly against;
  give information against
sentence give punishment from a
  court of law

193 **confirm** v.

verify

affirm state as a fact
bear witness to provide evidence of
  the truth
clinch settle something in a definite
  way, such as an argument or a deal
corroborate confirm formally,
  especially in law
sanction give approval to; authorize

194 **confused** adj.

bewildered   mixed up

baffled puzzled

muddled   mixed up mentally

all at sea   at a loss   in a stupor
mystified   non-plussed   perplexed

195   consult   v.
seek advice from

confer with   discuss; consult together

seek information from   seek the
opinion of

196   contact   v.

approach   communicate with
get in touch with   look up   notify

197   container   n.
receptacle

hamper   large basket with a lid
hopper   funnel through which grain
  or coal is passed
repository   place where things are
  stored
reservoir   place where liquid is stored,
  especially water for a city
vessel   receptacle for holding liquids

basin   basket   bin   bottle   bowl
box   dustbin   jar

198   contempt   n.
disdain

disrespect   rudeness
loathing   great hatred or disgust
scorn   open ridicule

disgust   revulsion

199   continual   adj.

frequent   recurrent   repeated

200   continuous   adj.

connected   constant   incessant
perpetual   unbroken   uninterrupted

201   convenient   adj.

handy   nearby   useful   within reach

202   cook   v.

barbecue   cook over an open fire on a
  metal frame
braise   cook slowly in a covered dish
broil   cook meat on a fire or gridiron
sauté   fry quickly in a little hot oil or
  fat
simmer   boil very gently
steam   cook above boiling water

roast

203   copy   n.
replica

carbon   exact copy made with carbon
  paper
counterfeit   close copy made in order
  to deceive
duplicate   one of two or more things
  that are exactly alike
forgery   exact copy made in order to
  defraud
imitation   something made to appear
  like something else
likeness   sameness in form;
  resemblance
semblance   outward appearance of,
  either real or pretended; a show

204   correct   adj.
accurate   right

factual   based on or containing facts
faithful   true to the facts or to an
  original
literal   following the usual meaning of
  the words

precise exact; correctly and clearly stated

unerring without making a mistake

205 corrupt adj.

immoral

deceitful not telling the truth

depraved having a bad character

dishonourable shameful

immoral lacking in, or not conforming to, accepted principles of what is right and wrong

perverted the opposite of what is regarded as normal or right

tainted infected with disease; moral decay

untrustworthy unreliable; undependable

bribable degenerate

206 crash n.

collapse collision smash-up

207 creep v.

crawl inch along move stealthily

208 cringe v.

cower bend down, especially in fear

fawn upon try to gain favour by over-praising and insincere attention

flinch draw back; wince

grovel be shamefully humble and eager to please

quail lose courage; give way before

recoil draw back suddenly in fear or disgust

shrink draw into oneself; cower

209 crisp adj.

abrupt sudden and unexpected; rough and impolite

brisk quick and active

concise brief, giving much information in few words

decisive showing firmness in settling something quickly

210 crockery n.

china collective name for thin, fine crockery

earthenware pots made of coarse baked clay

porcelain finest kind of china, thin and shiny

pottery handmade pots and other objects

stoneware heavy pottery made from clay containing flint

terracotta brownish-red unglazed pottery

211 crowd n.

throng

company number of guests: people combined together for business or trade

horde vast crowd

host large number of people or things

mob large, disorderly crowd of people

multitude very great number of things or people

audience body gang group rabble

212 cruel adj.

bloodthirsty eager for bloodshed

brutal merciless; very cruel

inhuman lacking normal human qualities of kindness, pity, sympathy and understanding

pitiless showing no tender human feeling

remorseless showing no sorrow for having done wrong

sadistic enjoying inflicting or watching cruelty
vicious morally evil; having a desire to hurt

implacable

213 cry v.

shed tears weep

blubber weep noisily
mourn grieve for a person who has died or for a thing lost
sob draw breath heavily and noisily while weeping
wail utter a long cry of grief or pain
whimper make feeble, frightened or complaining sounds
whine complain in a petty or feeble way

214 cunning adj.

artful crafty foxy sly wily

guileful full of deceitful tricks
scheming planning in a secret and underhand way
shrewd clever in judging what is to one's advantage

shifty tricky underhand

215 cut v.

carve cut in order to make a special shape; cut up meat
cleave divide by chopping; split along natural lines
dissect cut into parts in order to study
gash make a long, deep wound
slash cut with long forceful strokes with a knife, sword, or whip
slice cut cleanly into thin, flat pieces
slit make a narrow cut or opening

disjoint section sever sunder

216 daft adj.

addle-pated crack-brained crazy feather-brained half-baked mad as a hatter not all there senseless weak-minded

217 damp adj.

moist

clammy unpleasantly moist and sticky
dank unpleasantly cold and damp
humid damp air or climate
misty indistinct because of water vapour in the air
muggy unpleasantly warm and damp

drizzly steamy

218 danger n.

peril

hazard exposure to injury, loss, or evil
jeopardy danger of injury, loss, or death
menace threat of harm
risk possibility of meeting danger, suffering harm or loss
threat indication of something harmful or undesirable

219 dark adj.

dreary dull, sad and monotonous
funereal dark and mournful
gloomy almost dark; unlighted

220 dated adj.

out-of-date

obsolescent going out of use or fashion
obsolete no longer used
old-fashioned of a type no longer in style
passé past its, or his or her, prime

221 dawn n. (i)

daybreak

cockcrow crack-of-dawn
early light sunrise

222 dawn n. (ii)

beginning

advent coming of one who is awaited
arrival appearance of
emergence coming up, or out, or into
  view
inception beginning of the existence
  of something

awakening birth foundation

223 dazzle v.

blind take away the power of
  judgement
daze make unable to think or feel
  clearly
overawe fill with wonder and fear
stagger cause astonishment, worry,
  or confusion
stun shock into helplessness

amaze baffle bewilder disconcert
dumbfound nonplus strike dumb

224 dazzling adj.

overpowering extremely intense
resplendent gloriously bright and
  shiny

blinding brilliant

225 dead adj. (i)

deceased lifeless

defunct no longer existing or
  functioning
departed sympathetic word for the
  dead

extinct no longer existing in living
  form
inanimate showing no sign of life
perished having met a violent or
  untimely death

226 dead adj. (ii)

dead centre dead end dead level
dead silence

227 dear adj.

costly expensive highly-priced

228 deathless adj.

immortal imperishable undying

eternal existing always without
  beginning or end
everlasting never coming to an end
timeless independent of time
unending continuing for ever

historic

229 deceit n.

deception

dissimulation concealment of one's
  feelings and intentions
duplicity trickery by dishonest
  behaviour and dealing
fraud dishonest trick for the purpose
  of gain
hoax deceiving by way of a joke
swindle cheating in a business deal

double-dealing

230 decent adj.

respectable

befitting right and suitable
proper paying great attention to
  what is considered correct in society

obliging

231 decide v.

determine

adjudicate judge and pronounce a
 decision upon
arbitrate settle a dispute without bias
settle decide on, fix, or arrange

form an opinion   referee

232 decoration n.

adornment ornament; something
 adding beauty to
embellishment improvement by
 adding detail or ornament
ornament decorative object or detail

frill   nick-nack   trinket

233 defeat v.

beat

conquer overcome by force or effort
crush defeat and control completely
overrun spread over and occupy;
 devastate
overthrow remove from power;
 defeat
overwhelm overcome by force
 completely and suddenly
rout put to flight
subdue bring under control
vanquish defeat in a battle or contest

get the better of   thrash   trounce

234 defend v.

protect

safeguard protect from danger,
 damage, or injury
shield hide from harm or danger

speak up for   stand up for

235 define v.

explain exactly   outline clearly

characterize describe the essential
 qualities of
elucidate make clear; throw light on
 a problem

lay down   set out

236 defy v.

resist openly

challenge dare; threaten
confront face boldly or threateningly
deride laugh at scornfully
disobey not obey; go against
 someone's will or command
disregard pay no attention to; treat
 as of no importance
flout show contempt for

fly in the face of   scoff at

237 delay v.

put off   postpone

defer put off until later
detain keep waiting; cause delay to
hinder make it difficult for someone
 to do something
impede get in the way of
linger be slow in going
shelve put aside temporarily
suspend put off for a period

lag   slow up

238 delicious adj.

delectable highly enjoyable,
 especially to the taste
succulent juicy
toothsome of appetizing appearance,
 flavour or smell

appetizing   tasty

239 deny v.

disclaim say that one does not own or have any connection with
disprove show to be false or wrong
refute prove that a statement, opinion, or person is wrong
reject refuse to accept
repudiate refuse to acknowledge

disown *go without*

240 deserve v.

merit be worthy of

be entitled to *be qualified for*
have a claim to *have a right to*

241 destroy v.

wreck

demolish pull or knock down
devastate lay waste; cause great destruction to
gut remove or destroy the inside of a building
pulverize crush into powder
ravage do great damage to
wipe out destroy all of something

242 disgraceful adj.

shameful

contemptible deserving to be despised as worthless or bad
odious very offensive
sordid dirty and foul; not honourable

debased *repugnant* *shocking*

243 do v.

accomplish succeed in doing
achieve finish successfully; gain or reach by effort
act do what is required
develop bring to a later and more advanced stage; grow or cause to grow

discharge carry out a duty, promise, or contract
execute carry out an order or action; put a plan into effect
perform carry out a piece of work or an activity

244 doctor n.

consultant person qualified to give expert medical advice
general practitioner family doctor
physician specialist in medicine as distinct from a surgeon or family doctor
specialist person who is an expert in a special branch of medicine
surgeon doctor whose job is to perform medical operations

homeopath *osteopath*

245 dodge v.

avoid

duck lower oneself quickly to avoid being seen or hit
sidestep avoid by stepping sideways
veer change direction or course

dart aside *give the slip* *shy away*

246 drink v.

carouse have a merry drinking spree
gulp swallow drink or food hastily
guzzle drink or eat greedily
imbibe drink any form of alcohol
quaff drink heartily or in one long draught
swig swallow large mouthfuls
swill drink in large quantities
tipple be in the habit of drinking wine or spirits
toast honour or offer good wishes to someone by drinking

knock back *put away* *sip*

247 **droop** v.

sag

flag   become weak and less alive or
  active
languish   lose or lack will or strength;
  live under miserable conditions
slouch   stand, sit, or move in a tired-
  looking, round-shouldered way
slump   sit or flop down heavily and
  slackly
wilt   become limp from exhaustion or
  heat

stoop

248 **due** adj.

expected   *owing*   *payable*   *rightful*

249 **dull** adj.

boring   uninteresting

insipid   lacking in interest or liveliness
monotonous   lacking variety

dry as dust

250 **each** adj.

apiece   *for everyone*   *individually*
per   *to everyone*

251 **eagerly** adv.

enthusiastically   keenly

ardently   full of strong, warm feeling
avidly   greedily; wanting strongly
vehemently   showing a strong,
  intense feeling
zealously   full of hearty and persistent
  effort

heartily

252 **easily** adv.

effortlessly

by far   *probably*   *undoubtedly*

253 **eat** v.

chew   crush or grind with the teeth
devour   eat quickly with great
  hunger, or like a beast
dine   eat dinner; entertain to dinner
gorge   stuff oneself with food
masticate   chew food
munch   chew steadily and vigorously
nibble   take small, quick or gentle
  bites

bolt   *feast*   *glut*   *gobble up*
gulp down   *tuck in*   *wolf*

254 **edge** n.

border   boundary or frontier
boundary   limiting or dividing line
  between surfaces or spaces
brink   edge of a steep place or of a
  stretch of water
circumference   distance round an
  object or a place
fringe   edge of an area or group
margin   area on the outside edge of a
  larger area
perimeter   outer edge of any area
periphery   outside edge of an area;
  outer or surrounding region of area
verge   extreme edge

extremity   *limit*   *rim*   *side*

255 **effect** n.

outcome   result

aftermath   what follows after a bad
  event such as an accident
consequence   result of
issue   outcome; point in question
sequel   what follows or arises out of
  an earlier event
upshot   final result

256 **efficient** adj.

adept   highly skilled

capable   having the ability to do something satisfactorily
competent   having sufficient skill or knowledge; capable
expert   having great knowledge or skill
trained   able and accustomed to do something through being taught

masterly

257   effort   n.

application   careful and continuous attention or effort
grind   hard, uninteresting work
striving   struggle towards something
struggle   vigorous effort; hard contest
toil   long work needing great effort

exertion   *trouble*

258   elsewhere   adv.

somewhere else

absent   *away*   *not here*   *not present*

259   emphasize   v.

stress

belabour   talk about at unnecessary length
bring home   convince
dramatize   present in a striking or exciting manner
feature   give special prominence to
highlight   draw special attention to
mark   notice; watch carefully
underline   state forcibly; reinforce

rub in

260   empty   adj.

unfurnished   unsupplied with what is necessary for some purpose
unoccupied   without anyone or anything in it

vacant   not filled or being used
barren   bereft of

261   end   n. (i)

close   conclusion   finish

expiration   end of a period of time
finale   final section of a musical composition or a drama
terminus   last stop on a railway or bus route

extremity   *termination*   *winding-up*

262   end   n. (ii)

purpose   thing intended; object to be attained

aim   *goal*   *object*   *objective*

263   enemy   n.

foe

adversary   person or group one is opposed to
antagonist   one who is actively hostile or opposed to someone or something
assailant   person who attacks another, either by actions or words
attacker   person who starts a fight
opponent   person who takes the opposite side

264   energy   n.

vigour

drive   strong urge and will to do things
effectiveness   ability or power to do what is necessary
stamina   staying-power; ability to withstand prolonged physical or mental strain
virility   masculine vigour, strength and power
vitality   liveliness; ability to endure

elbow grease

265 **engine** n.

dynamo small machine turning mechanical energy into electricity
generator apparatus for converting mechanical energy into electrical energy, or for producing a gas
machine man-made instrument for applying mechanical power
motor machine that changes power into movement
transformer apparatus for changing electrical voltage
turbine machine or motor that is driven by a wheel that is itself turned by a flow of water or gas

266 **enjoyable** adj.

amusing delightful diverting entertaining pleasurable satisfying

267 **enough** adj.

adequate sufficient

ample more than enough

268 **escape** v.

get away

abscond go away suddenly and secretly, especially after wrongdoing
elude escape skilfully or by means of a trick
evade avoid by cleverness or trickery
flee

269 **essential** adj.

indispensable necessary vital

basic fundamental

270 **even** adj.

flat level

consistent unchanging; having a regular pattern or style
equable free from extremes; uniform
unvaried staying the same

unchanging

271 **event** n.

affair happening incident occasion occurrence

272 **evidently** adv.

as far as one can see clearly obviously plainly seemingly

273 **examine** v.

inspect

analyse separate into parts to find out about
cross-question question closely to test answers to previous questions
probe search into or question closely
scrutinize look at in minute detail
sound out try to find out the opinion or intention of

test

274 **example** n.

exemplar model; person or thing to be imitated
pattern excellent example to be followed
sample typical small quantity
specimen single typical thing, especially one chosen for showing or testing
standard level of quality considered acceptable

illustration instance precedent

275 **except** prep.

apart from barring but excluding not counting omitting

276 excess n.

surfeit

abundance plentiful supply
glut larger supply or quantity than
  can be used
surplus amount additional to what is
  needed or used; what is left over

plethora superabundance

277 exchange v.

barter trade by exchanging goods for
  other goods, not for money
interchange give and receive one
  thing for another
substitute put or use one thing
  instead of another
swap trade one small thing for
  another
trade buy, sell, or exchange

278 exciting adj.

*fascinating irresistible mind-
boggling rousing startling*

279 expect v.

anticipate regard as likely to happen
count on depend on; rely on
foresee be aware of or realize a thing
  beforehand

await

280 experienced adj.

practised

competent able to do what is needed
proficient doing something correctly
  and satisfactorily through training
  or practice
qualified having the abilities,
  qualities and skills necessary to do a
  particular job

well-grounded

281 explain v.

make plain

clarify make more easily understood
define state or explain the meaning
  precisely
expound set forth or explain in detail
interpret understand or show the
  meaning of
unfold make clear step by step

account for clear up spell out

282 explore v.

prospect explore in search of
  something, such as gold or oil
reconnoitre make a preliminary
  survey, usually of an enemy's
  position
survey look at and take a general
  view of

283 fabulous adj.

*amazing astounding extraordinary
fantastic inconceivable marvellous
miraculous unbelievable wonderful*

284 face n.

countenance expression of the face
expression look that shows one's
  feelings
features any of the named parts of
  the face
lineaments facial outline or
  distinctive characteristic
physiognomy features or expressions
  considered as showing personality
visage appearance and aspect of the
  face

285 fact n.

detail factor item point truth

286 fade v.

blanch become pale or white
bleach whiten by sunlight or
 chemicals
dim become indistinct and not clearly
 seen
disappear cease to be visible

cloud   decrease   grow dull

287 faint adj. (i)

*dim   faded   indistinct   obscure
vague*

288 faint adj. (ii)

*dizzy   exhausted   faint-hearted
giddy*

289 fair adj.

just   unbiased   unprejudiced

detached not influenced by feelings
 or other people's opinions
disinterested acting fairly because not
 influenced by personal advantage
dispassionate free from emotion and
 fair in judgement
equitable reasonable and just
even-handed treating everyone
 equally
impartial not favouring one more
 than another

above board

290 faithful adj.

loyal

devoted very loyal or loving
dedicated devoting one's time and
 energy to a special purpose
patriotic loyally supporting one's
 country and its way of life
staunch dependably firm in attitude
steadfast firm; not changing or giving
 way

291 fake adj.

sham

counterfeit made exactly like
 something real in order to deceive
forged imitating for dishonest gain
fraudulent acting with intent to
 deceive
imitating copying the appearance
spurious not what it claims to be

pseudo

292 false adj.

untrue

bogus pretended
ersatz used in imitation of the real
 thing
fictitious untrue; invented
insincere not genuine in feeling,
 manner or actions
mendacious telling lies; untruthful
trumped up invented or dishonest
 excuse or accusation

assumed   phoney

293 fame n.

renown

acclaim enthusiastic shout or
 demonstration of welcome or
 approval
celebrity state of being well known;
 well-known person
eminence position of superiority;
 distinction or high rank
notoriety state of being widely and
 unfavourably known
prestige respect and influence
 resulting from a good reputation
 and/or past achievements
prominence importance; being
 outstanding
reputation what is generally said or
 believed about a person or thing
stardom position of being a top
 performer

294 famous adj.

renowned   well-known

distinguished   outstanding for excellence
esteemed   thought very highly of
illustrious   very well known for great works

popular

295 fan n.

devotee   enthusiast   follower

admirer   person who regards another with pleasure, approval and respect
aficionado   keen and knowledgeable follower of a particular sport or pastime
champion   person who fights, argues or speaks in support of another, or of a cause
fanatic   person whose enthusiasm for something is beyond normal limits
partisan   strong and often uncritical supporter of a person, group, or cause
zealot   extremely enthusiastic and devoted supporter of a cause, especially a religious one

296 fantastic adj. (i)

*illusory   unreal   outlandish
visionary   whimsical*

297 fantastic adj. (ii)

excellent   fabulous   wonderful

298 far adj.

distant

far-flung   at or spread over a great distance
inaccessible   unable to be reached
remote   far away in place or time

back of beyond   god-forsaken

299 far-fetched adj.

*improbable   incredible   strained
unlikely   unnatural*

300 farm n.

croft   small enclosed field, next to a house, worked by the family
grange   country house with farm buildings that belong to it
hacienda   ranch or large estate in Spanish-speaking countries
homestead   farmhouse or similar building with the land and buildings round it
manor   large country house or the landed estate belonging to it
ranch   very large farm where sheep, cattle, horses, or other animals are bred
smallholding   piece of land of more than one acre in area, but usually less than 50 acres, sold or let for cultivation

301 fashion n. (i)

mode   style

craze   very popular fashion lasting only a short time
fad   short-lived but keenly followed interest or practice
trend-setter   person who leads the way in fashion
vogue   generally accepted fashion or custom at a certain time

fashion n. (ii)

manner   way

302 fast adj.

quick   rapid   speedy   swift

303 fasten v.

bond hold together, usually by glue
clamp hold things firmly by turning a screw
clasp grasp, hold, or embrace closely
clip fix or fasten with a small plastic or metal object
hitch fasten with a loop or hook
mitre join two pieces of wood or cloth so that their ends form a right angle
solder join metal parts together with a soft melted alloy
tack fasten with a small nail; sew temporarily with loose stitches
tether fasten an animal with a rope or chain to limit its movements

attach cement glue

304 fat adj.

obese

chubby having a round, usually pleasing, form
corpulent having a bulky body
flabby having too soft flesh
overweight weighing more than is normal or required
paunchy having a protruding belly
plump having a full, rounded shape
podgy short and fat
portly stout and dignified
stout solidly built and rather fat
tubby shaped like a tub

gross pot-bellied

305 fatal adj. (i)

deadly lethal mortal

toxic of, related to, or caused by poison
venomous poisonous; full of bitter feeling or hatred
virulent very powerful and dangerous; strongly and bitterly hostile

306 fatal adj. (ii)

disastrous

detrimental causing harm or damage
injurious hurtful; abusive or slanderous

calamitous catastrophic ruinous

307 fearful adj.

appalling shocking
dreadful very bad indeed; very shocking
frightful causing horror; ugly
terrible causing terror; very bad or incompetent
terrifying filling with very great fear

atrocious ghastly hideous

308 feather n.

crest tuft of feathers on a bird's head or on a helmet
down very fine, soft, furry feathers or short hairs
pinion end part of a bird's wing; the flight feathers
plumage general name for a bird's feathers
plume feather, especially a large or ornamental one
quill one of the large feathers on a bird's wing or tail

309 feed v.

board be supplied with daily meals in return for payment or services
browse feed as animals do, on leaves or grass
crop bite off and eat the crops of grass or plants grown as feed
foster promote the growth or development
graze eat growing grass
nourish keep alive and well by means of food
nurture care for, feed, and rear

310 feeling n.

consciousness state of mental awareness of oneself and one's surroundings
emotion instinctive feeling, such as love, hate, or grief
impression effect produced on the mind
inkling slight knowledge or suspicion; hint
intuition power of knowing or understanding something immediately without reasoning or being taught
passion intense emotion or obsession
premonition feeling that something is going to happen, usually unwelcome
sensation direct feeling, as of heat or pain, from the senses

foreboding *intimation* *presentiment*

311 few adj.

hardly any not many scarcely any some

meagre not enough in quantity, quality, or strength
scanty hardly enough
scarce not much or many compared with what is wanted
skimpy spending, providing, or using less than is really needed

312 fierce adj.

brutish very rough or very cruel
ferocious savagely fierce or cruel
murderous very dangerous, difficult, or unpleasant
savage uncontrollable and fiercely cruel
violent involving great force or strength
wild lacking restraint, discipline, or control

313 fight n.

affray fight in public between small groups
battle fight between large organized forces
bout boxing match
combat contest between two individuals, or two military forces
duel fight with guns or swords between two people

conflict *tussle*

314 find v.

chance upon *come across*
come upon *discover* *happen upon*
hit upon *light upon* *locate*

315 fine adj.

first-class *first-rate* *splendid*

316 finish v.

complete conclude end
get through terminate

achieve gain by effort
accomplish succeed in doing
seal settle solemnly

fulfil *round off*

317 fire n.

blaze bright flame or fire
combustion catching fire and burning
conflagration great and destructive fire
holocaust great destruction or loss of life, especially by fire

318 first adj.

best of the highest quality, value, or use

earliest first to arrive
foremost most important; leading; furthest forward
initial of or belonging to the beginning
original new in character or design
primary earliest in time or order; first in a series
principal chief; first in rank or importance

opening premier

319 **fitting** adj.

suitable

adapted changed for a new use or situation
appropriate right for its purpose
apt exactly suitable for the circumstance or purpose
compatible able to exist or be used together
pertinent to the point
seemly in accordance with the accepted standards of good taste

opportune

320 **flag** n.

banner strip of cloth with a sign, carried between two poles in a procession
Blue Peter blue flag with a white square hoisted by a ship about to sail
colours flag of a regiment or ship
ensign flag flown by a ship to show what nation she belongs to
pennant long, narrow, pointed flag
standard distinctive flag used at ceremonies
tricolour flag with three colours in stripes; French national flag

321 **flat** adj.

level

horizontal in a flat position, along or parallel to the ground
prone lying flat
prostrate stretched out face downwards
reclining lying back
unbroken not interrupted by humps or ridges

322 **flatter** v.

compliment express admiration; congratulate
fawn try to win favour by overpraising or being insincerely attentive
praise speak favourably and with admiration
toady to be too nice to someone to gain personal advantage

pander to

323 **flow** v.

cascade pour or fall in quantity
flood fill or become covered with water; overflow
glide move noiselessly in a smooth, continuous and effortless manner
gush flow or pour out suddenly
jet shoot out forcefully from a small opening
ripple form very small waves like wrinkles
rush move suddenly with great speed
spout come or pour out in a forceful stream
surge move forward like powerful waves
trickle flow or cause to flow in drops or a thin stream

324 flower n.

bloom

annual plant that lives for only one
year or season
biennial plant that lives for two
years, flowering and dying in the
second
blossom mass of flowers appearing
on a tree or bush
bouquet bunch of flowers for
carrying in the hand
floret small flower, especially one
making up the head of a composite
flower, e.g., a daisy
nosegay small bunch of flowers,
usually worn on a dress
perennial plant living for several
years

325 flying adj.

drifting driven along as if by wind or
waves
flapping waving slowly up and down
or to and fro, making a noise
floating held up freely in air, gas, or
liquid without sinking
fluttering moving the wings hurriedly
in flying or trying to fly
gliding flying without engine power
hanging remaining in the air
hovering staying in the air in one
place
planing flying without moving wings
or using engines
skimming moving lightly and quickly
near or just touching a surface
soaring rising high in flight
zooming moving quickly, especially
with a buzzing sound

326 former adj.

previous

earlier   late   one-time   past

327 found v.

create cause something new to exist;
produce something new
establish set up on a permanent basis
institute set up for the first time
originate begin or cause to begin
set up begin a new venture
start up set in motion; begin an
activity

328 frank adj.

blunt rough and plain, without
trying to be polite or kind
candid directly truthful, even when
the truth is unwelcome
forthright direct and short in manner
and speech
guileless lacking in cunning or deceit

*artless   outspoken   plain-spoken
straight-forward   uninhibited*

329 freely adv.

readily   unreservedly

generously given readily and in large
amounts
independently done on one's own
without help from others
informally without ceremony
naturally without trying to look or
sound different from usual
voluntarily willingly and without
payment

330 friend n.

accomplice partner in wrongdoing
ally person who helps and supports
another
chum close friend
companion person who escorts,
attends or spends time with another
comrade friend and/or equal in
work, play or war

crony   pal of long standing

collaborator   *confederate*

331   **frown**   v.

glower   scowl sullenly
grimace   twist the face in pain or
  disgust, or to cause amusement

look black   *look daggers*

332   **full**   adj.

filled

brimming   full to the top
chock-a-block   crammed or crowded
  together
gorged   choked up; stuffed full
satiated   cloyed with an excess of
  something

crammed   *glutted*   *jam-packed*

333   **fun**   n.

*amusement   clowning   enjoyment
entertainment   fooling   gaiety
joking   jollity   merriment   mirth
play   playfulness   recreation
relaxation   teasing*

334   **funny**   adj.

amusing   causing to laugh or smile
comical   amusing in an odd way
diverting   entertaining
hilarious   extremely funny
humorous   appealing to one's sense of
  fun
side-splitting   causing uncontrollable
  laughter

jocular   *ludicrous*

335   **fuss**   n.

bother   pother

commotion   noisy confusion or
  excitement
flurry   state of troubled hurry and
  excitement
fluster   state of being hot, nervous,
  and confused

336   **game**   n.

competition   friendly contest in which
  people try to do better than their
  rivals
contest   formal game between two or
  more people or teams
diversion   entertainment
match   game or sports event
regatta   races between rowing or
  sailing boats
sport   physical outdoor or indoor
  game with rules
tournament   contest of skill between
  players involving a series of matches

337   **gasp**   v.

exclaim   utter suddenly because of
  strong feeling or pain
gulp   make a sudden swallowing
  movement of surprise or nervousness
heave   pant; strain one's throat as if
  vomiting
snort   make a rough noise by blowing
  air down the nose

338   **gentle**   adj.

mild

compassionate   feeling pity and
  wishing to help others or show mercy
considerate   taking care not to
  inconvenience or hurt others
tender   easily moved to pity or
  sympathy
thoughtful   showing thought for the
  needs of others

soothing   *tender-hearted*

339 get v.

obtain

acquire gain possession of by one's own efforts

appropriate take and use as one's own without permission

benefit be given something useful, profitable, or helpful

come by obtain something, especially accidentally; find

fetch go for and bring back

gain get through one's own efforts something desirable

inherit receive property, a title, or possessions from someone who has died

procure obtain by care or effort

receive accept or take in something offered, sent, or given

secure become the possessor of, especially as the result of effort

seize take possession of by force or official order

take lay hold of; gain possession of by force or effort

earn *pocket* *purchase* *take home*

340 gift n. (i)

present

bequest money, articles, or property left to someone in a will

contribution something given or supplied jointly with others

donation gift of money to a fund or institution

dowry property or money brought by a bride to her husband

endowment source of income

inheritance thing received from someone who has died

offering contribution for a religious purpose

voucher kind of ticket that can be exchanged for certain goods or services

alms *dole* *gratuity* *tip*

341 gift n. (ii)

talent

bent natural skill or liking

flair natural aptitude to do something easily or select what is good

genius exceptional great inborn ability

342 girl n.

adolescent young person between 13 and 16

child young female below the age of puberty

juvenile young person

maid female servant doing indoor work

maiden unmarried girl

minor person not yet reached the age at which she is responsible in law for her actions

tomboy girl who enjoys boyish recreations

lass *lassie* *maidservant* *minx* *miss* *wench*

343 give v.

bestow

allocate give as a share of something available; set aside for a particular purpose

assign set apart for a particular function or event

award give by official decision as a payment, penalty, or prize

contribute supply something jointly with others

dispense deal out

donate make a gift to a fund or institution

present give away, especially at a ceremonial occasion

allot *consign* *offer* *yield*

344 glad adj.
well-pleased

delighted greatly pleased
elated filled with pride and joy
thrilled filled with emotion and
excitement

gratified pleased as punch

345 gladly adv.

*cheerfully smilingly ungrudgingly
willingly with good grace
with pleasure*

346 glass n.

beaker tall drinking-cup, often
without a handle
chalice vessel like a large goblet for
holding wine
goblet drinking-glass with stem, foot
and no handles
tumbler flat-bottomed drinking-glass
with no handle or stem
wineglass glass, usually rounded,
with a stem and base, for drinking
wine from

347 go v.

advance move forward
decamp leave any place suddenly and
secretly
depart go away from; leave
embark put or go on board ship at
the start of a journey
make away go away in haste; steal or
abduct

progress set out travel

348 good adj. (i)
virtuous

devout earnestly religious

honourable deserving respect
because of good character
moral right and just
noble possessing excellent qualities,
especially of character

high-minded righteous saintly

349 good adj. (ii)
beneficial causing a good result
desirable what is wanted
passable just good enough to be
accepted
suitable good for its purpose

350 goods n.

chattels movable possessions
commodities useful things; articles of
trade
merchandise goods for sale or trade
wares manufactured goods offered
for sale

paraphernalia produce stock

351 grasp v. (i)
clasp clench grip seize

apprehend arrest and take into
custody
clutch hold tightly
grapple seize and struggle with
hold take and keep in one's arms,
hands, or teeth
nab seize as a thief
snatch take quickly or when a chance
occurs

352 grasp v. (ii)
comprehend

apprehend grasp the meaning of;
understand
realize understand and believe
something

353 grass n.

green smooth stretch of grass for a special purpose
hay grass mown and dried for cattle food
herbage grass and other field plants
lawn area of closely-cut grass in a garden or park
meadow field of grass to make hay from
pasture land covered with grass and similar plants suitable for grazing cattle
turf soil with grass and roots growing in it

354 grassland n.

downs low rounded hills covered with grass, usually of chalk
heath area of flat, uncultivated land with low shrubs
moor wide, open, often raised area covered with heather, rough grass, and bushes
pampas large, grassy, treeless plains in South America
prairie large, treeless tract of land, especially in North America
savannah grassy plain in hot regions, with few or no trees
steppe large area of plain without trees in South-East Europe and Siberia
tundra vast, level, treeless Arctic regions where the subsoil is frozen
veld high, flat, open grassland in South Africa
wold area of open upland country

355 grave adj.

serious

grim stern in appearance
sedate dignified and not easily troubled
solemn not smiling or cheerful; dignified and impressive

sombre sadly serious
staid steady and unexciting in manner and taste

unsmiling

356 greedy adj. (i)

acquisitive keen to collect and own things
avaricious extremely greedy for riches
grasping avaricious; miserly
mercenary working only for money or other reward
rapacious taking everything one can, especially by force
venal easily bribed or corrupted

greedy adj. (ii)

gluttonous eating excessively

357 grey adj.

*ashen   dove-grey   gunmetal-grey
leaden   pearly   silvery   smoky*

358 guard v.

keep safe   protect   watch over

conduct lead or guide
defend protect against attack
escort accompany as an honour, guide, protection, or to prevent escape
police control by, or as if, using police
shield protect or hide from harm, danger, or discovery

359 guess v.

conjecture

estimate calculate the value of something
reckon have as one's opinion

suppose take as likely; consider as true or probable

surmise give as a reasonable guess

speculate

360 **gun** n.

firearm

automatic weapon that can be fired repeatedly by pressure on the trigger

blunderbuss old type of gun with wide mouth, firing many balls at one shot

cannon old type of large, heavy gun firing solid metal balls; automatic aircraft gun of large calibre

carbine short, light automatic rifle of limited range

Colt heavy revolver firing six bullets

howitzer short, heavy gun firing shells high over a short distance

machine-gun rapid-firing automatic gun, usually mounted, firing small ammunition

mortar short, heavy gun for firing shells at a high angle

musket early long-barrelled gun used before the invention of the rifle

pistol small hand-gun

revolver pistol with a revolving barrel

rifle gun with long grooved barrel, fired from the shoulder

shotgun gun for firing small shot at close range

361 **habit** n.

addiction state of being utterly dependent on some habit, especially taking drugs

custom usual way of behaving or doing something

dependence condition of needing the help of and unable to do without

groove a way of living that has become a habit; a rut

practice habitual course of action that is accepted as correct

rut habitual, usually dull, way of life

usage customary manner of using or treating something

mania *weakness for*

362 **hair** n.

curls coiled locks of hair

down very fine, soft short hairs

fleece woolly hair of a sheep or similar animal

fur soft, thick fine hair covering the bodies of certain animals

hide animal skin, especially when used for leather

mane long hair on a horse's or lion's neck

pelt animal skin, especially with the fur or hair still on it

ringlets long, hanging curls of hair

shock bushy, untidy mass of hair

thatch thick growth of hair on the head

tress lock or plait of woman's hair

tonsure

363 **hang** v.

dangle hang or swing loosely

droop bend or hang downwards

string up hang something high; kill by hanging

suspend hang from above

364 **happen** v.

occur take place

chance take place by accident

come about happen in due course of time

crop up arise unexpectedly

befall *transpire*

365 happening n.

event   incident   occurrence

accident   something, especially
  something unpleasant or damaging,
  happening unexpectedly or by chance
circumstance   one of the conditions or
  facts connected with an event or
  person
mishap   unfortunate happening,
  usually not of a serious nature
phenomenon   fact or event as it
  appears to the senses; remarkable
  person, thing or event

366 hardly adv.

barely   scarcely

367 hastily adv.

hurriedly

headlong   falling or plunging
  forwards; in a hasty or rash way
precipitately   rashly, hurriedly,
  and/or inconsiderately
promptly   without delay

368 hat n.

beret   round, soft flat cap with no
  peak
boater   hard flat straw hat
bonnet   hat with strings that tie under
  the chin
bowler   hard felt hat with rounded
  top and brim, usually black
busby   tall fur helmet worn by the
  Guards on ceremonial occasions
cap   soft, flat head-covering without a
  brim but often with a peak
fez   man's high, round flat-topped red
  cap with a tassel, worn by Muslims
head-dress   ornamental covering or
  band worn on the head
mitre   tall head-dress worn by bishops
  and abbots as a symbol of office

panama   hat of fine pliant straw-like
  material
stetson   hat with wide brim and high
  crown worn by cowboys
top hat   man's tall, stiff silk, black or
  grey hat worn with formal dress
topper   another word for top hat
toque   woman's close-fitting brimless
  hat with a high crown
trilby   man's soft felt hat with a
  lengthwise dent in the crown and a
  narrow brim

369 hate v

loathe

abhor   feel very great hatred
abominate   have great hatred and
  dislike for
despise   regard as inferior or
  worthless
detest   dislike strongly
execrate   curse; feel or express hatred

370 have v.

own   possess, belong to
retain   keep in one's possession or use;
  not lose

possess

371 heap n.

pile

accumulation   an increasing quantity
hoard   carefully saved and guarded
  store
load   amount that can be carried
mass   great quantity
stack   orderly pile
supply   stock or store; amount of
  something

batch   clump   cluster   collection

372 heartless adj.

cold-hearted hardened hard-hearted uncaring unfeeling unsympathetic

373 hearty adj.

affable showing warmth and friendliness
bouncy lively in manner and movement
buoyant light-hearted, cheerful, and hopeful
cordial good-tempered and friendly
whole-hearted with all one's ability, interest, and sincerity
zestful full of enthusiasm and enjoyment

374 help v.

aid assist

abet encourage or give help to a crime or criminal
accommodate oblige or do a favour for
collaborate work in partnership
contribute help to bring about
cooperate work or act together for a purpose
expedite make a plan or arrangement go faster
facilitate make easy or easier

befriend lend a hand succour

375 hide v.

conceal secrete

camouflage disguise or conceal objects by colouring or covering them, so that they blend into their surroundings
disguise change the appearance of
enshroud cover completely and hide

screen shelter, conceal, or protect
veil partly conceal

376 hill n.

bluff broad, steep headland, bank, or cliff
dune sand-hill piled up by wind on the seashore or in a desert
eminence piece of rising ground
foothill one of the low hills near the bottom of a mountain or range
hummock hump in the ground
knoll small, rounded hill
mound small hill; mass of piled-up earth or stones
tor prominent rock or heap of rocks, especially on a hill

377 hit v.

strike

batter hit hard and often
beat strike repeatedly, especially with a stick
belabour beat severely
bludgeon hit repeatedly with a heavy-headed stick
buffet hit, especially with the fist
clout give a hard blow with the hand
cuff strike lightly with the open hand
flay strip off the skin by whipping
flick strike or remove with a quick, light blow
flog beat severely with a whip or stick as a punishment
knock strike with a noisy, sharp blow
pummel hit repeatedly, especially with the fists
punch strike a quick, strong blow with the closed fist
scourge beat with a whip
slap strike quickly with the open hand

tap knock gently; strike lightly
thrash beat thoroughly; hit with
  repeated blows

club   rap   spank

378 **holiday** n.

vacation

fête outdoor entertainment, usually
  to raise funds
festival religious or other celebration
field-day day of much activity,
  especially of brilliant and exciting
  events
gala joyous and festive organized
  occasion
jamboree noisy, happy party

recess

379 **home** n.

abode dwelling place; house
accommodation living premises
apartment room or set of rooms for
  living in
bungalow one-storeyed house
cottage small, simple house usually
  in the country
domicile dwelling-place; home
dwelling place to live in
habitation place to live in
housing estate number of houses in
  an area planned as a unit
lodgings room or rooms, not in a
  hotel, rented for living in
residence place where one resides or
  lives, especially a grand one
rooms set of rooms occupied by a
  person or family

*flat   caravan   house   maisonette
pad   penthouse   shack   shanty
tenement*

380 **homely** adj.

plain

unaffected natural in behaviour or
  character
unsophisticated simple in ways and
  tastes

381 **horse** n.

Arab small, fast, intelligent breed of
  horse, originally from Arabia, used
  mainly for riding
bronco wild or half-tamed horse of
  western North America
Clydesdale heavy powerful breed of
  carthorse, originally from Scotland
cob sturdy, short-legged horse for
  riding
mustang small, wild horse of Mexico
  and south-west U.S.A.
nag horse spoken of in a slighting
  way
piebald horse with irregular patches
  of white and black or other dark
  colour
shire large powerful English
  carthorse
skewbald horse marked or spotted in
  white and any colour except black
thoroughbred bred of pure or
  pedigree stock

382 **however** adv.

*all the same   even so
in whatever way   nevertheless
to whatever extent*

383 **hurt** v.

injure damage
ache suffer a continuous dull pain
burn injure by fire or acid; be
  unpleasantly hot

smart   feel a stinging pain, not lasting long
sting   feel or cause to feel sharp pain in one particular place
throb   giving pain in a strong, quick, steady rhythm
wound   injure by a cut, stab, blow or tear

bruise

384   **idea**   n.

conception   act of forming an idea or plan
impression   uncertain idea, belief, or remembrance
notion   vague idea or opinion, often incorrect
theory   reasonable explanation of something for which certain proof is still needed
viewpoint   way of considering or judging a thing or person

385   **if**   conj.

even though   granting
in the event that   on condition
providing   supposing   whether

386   **ignore**   v.
disregard   take no notice of

brush aside   reject casually or curtly
cold-shoulder   treat with deliberate unfriendliness
neglect   give no or too little attention or care to
omit   leave not done or fail to do
slight   treat rudely, without respect, or as if unimportant
snub   reject or humiliate a person by treating him scornfully
turn a blind eye   know what is happening, but choose to ignore it

387   **ill**   adj.

poorly   sick   sickly   unwell

ailing   unwell, especially over a long period
diseased   affected with an unhealthy condition
indisposed   slightly ill
infirm   weak in body or mind, especially from age or illness
unhealthy   not having or not showing good health

bedridden   laid up

388   **imaginary**   adj.

fanciful   using the imagination freely
illusory   deceiving and unreal

389   **improve**   v. (i)
make better

rectify   put right
redress   put right a wrong or an injustice
reform   make or become better by removing faults
regenerate   make better morally; give new life or vigour to

reconstruct   remodel   reorganize

improve   v. (ii)
get better

recover

390   **in**   prep.

during   in the midst of
in the thick of   on the inside of
within

391   **inaudible**   adj.

faint   not clearly heard

imperceptible too slight to be heard
indistinct not able to be heard clearly
muted deadened or muffled
unclear not able to be understood

392 incidentally adv.

by the way

casually *in passing*

393 increase v.

enlarge make greater

amass gather in great amounts
amplify make fuller, larger, or
greater; add details to
augment increase in size, amount, or
quality
expand make or grow larger
extend make longer in space or time;
increase the scope of
supplement make additions to

394 incurable adj.

fatal causing or ending in death
inoperable unable to be cured by
surgery
terminal related to an illness that will
cause death

395 indeed adv.

admittedly *assuredly* *in fact*
in truth *really* *truly*

396 indirect adj.

circuitous roundabout
divergent going in different
directions from a point
erratic irregular or uneven
meandering wandering in a leisurely,
aimless way
out-of-the-way distant; uncommon

tortuous full of twists and turns; not
straightforward

wandering zigzag

397 individual adj.

characteristic typical or distinctive
distinct definite and unmistakable
inherent forming a natural part of
personal belonging to oneself

398 indulgent adj.

complacent self-satisfied
forgiving ceasing to feel angry or
bitter towards
lax careless or lazy; not strict or
severe
lenient merciful, especially when
awarding punishment
permissive allowing a great deal of,
or too much, freedom
tolerant able to put up with the
beliefs, actions, or opinions of
others without protest

self-gratifying *spoilt*

399 infamous adj.

of ill repute

notorious widely and unfavourably
known
reprehensible deserving to be blamed
or scolded
scandalous shocking to feelings of
what is right or proper

abhorrent

400 infect v.

blight spoil plants through disease
causing withering
contaminate make impure by mixing
with dirty or poisonous matter
corrupt turn from good to bad
degrade change from a higher to a

lower kind of living matter; change
for the worse
pollute   make dirty or impure,
especially by adding harmful or
offensive substances
taint   affect with a trace of some bad
quality, decay, or infection

401   insist   v.

assert   state forcibly
claim   demand as the rightful owner
or one's right; state as a fact
declare   state with great force; make
known publicly or officially
emphasize   give special importance to
certain words or details
maintain   assert as true

402   inspire   v.

animate   bring or give life
exhilarate   make very happy or lively
impress   make a person form a strong,
usually favourable, opinion of
something
invigorate   give new strength and
courage to

hearten   *uplift*

403   instant   adj.

instantaneous   occurring or done at
once

expeditious   *immediate*   *prompt*

404   instead   adv.

as an alternative to
as a substitute for   *in place of*
in preference to   *preferably*
rather than

405   intact   adj.

complete   *sound*   *unchanged*
undamaged   *untouched*   *whole*

406   intend   v.

contemplate   think about, have in
view as a possibility
propose   declare as one's plan; suggest
resolve   decide firmly
scheme   plan in a secret or underhand
way

aim at   *aspire to*   *have in mind*   *plan*

407   interesting   adj.

absorbing   taking all one's attention
engrossing   occupying one's attention
completely
fascinating   having great attraction
intriguing   rousing curiosity
riveting   holding firmly, usually in
fascinated attention or horror

diverting   *entertaining*   *spell-binding*
thought-provoking

408   invent   v.

devise

compose   make up or form; write
music, poetry, or stories
create   bring into existence; produce
design   draw or plan out for a specific
purpose
discover   find out or find, especially
for the first time

conjure up

409   island   n.

isle

archipelago   group of many small
islands
atoll   ring-shaped coral reef enclosing
a lagoon
islet   small island
reef   line of rocks, coral, or sand at,
or near, the surface of the sea

410 jab v.

dig poke, especially in the ribs
elbow push with one's elbows
prod push with a finger or pointed
  object
thrust push forcibly and suddenly as
  with a sword or knife

411 jagged adj.

notched having V-shaped cuts or
  indentations
ragged torn or frayed
ridged formed into narrow, raised
  strips
serrated having a series of small
  projections like the teeth of a saw
uneven not level or smooth; varying

craggy saw-toothed

412 jail n.

gaol prison

detention centre place where young
  offenders may be kept for short
  periods
lock-up room or small building
  where prisoners can be kept for a
  short time
penal institution place of punishment
  awarded by law
penitentiary State or federal prison in
  America
police station office of a local police
  force

413 jaunty adj.

bouncy self-confident

buoyant light-hearted and cheerful
sprightly gay and light in manner and
  movement

eager jolly

414 jealous adj.

covetous desiring eagerly, especially
  something belonging to another
  person
envious feeling discontented about
  someone else's qualities or possessions
possessive unwilling to share one's
  things with other people

green-eyed suspicious

415 job n.

work

chore small, routine and tedious
  task especially a domestic one
employment work done to earn a
  living
livelihood way one earns enough to
  pay for what is necessary
occupation activity that keeps a
  person busy; one's employment
office position of authority or trust
trade business, especially buying,
  selling, or exchanging products or
  goods
vocation urge to follow a particular
  career, especially one to serve others

appointment

416 join v.

connect join, link or fasten together
fasten make or become firmly fixed
  or closed
link make or be a connection
  between
splice join by overlapping or weaving
  ends together
unite make or become one

bolt together chain rivet weld

417 joke n.

jest

chestnut stale old joke or story

gag   joke or funny story, especially as part of a comedian's act
quip   witty or sarcastic remark
wisecrack   quick, short, clever remark
witticism   sharp, funny, intelligent remark

spoof   whimsy

418   journey   n.

excursion   short journey for pleasure
expedition   journey or voyage for a particular purpose
globe-trotting   travelling all over the world, especially as a tourist
jaunt   short trip, especially one taken for pleasure
outing   short outward and return journey for pleasure
pilgrimage   journey made to a place as a mark of respect
quest   journey in search of something
safari   trip to hunt or explore, especially in East Africa
tour   journey through a country, town or building; visiting various places or things of interest
trek   long and often difficult journey
trip   any tour or journey, especially for pleasure
voyage   journey, especially a long one by sea or air

cruise

419   jump   v.

leapfrog   jump astride over someone's back; overtake one after the other
pounce   spring or swoop down on and grasp
vault   jump over, using the hands or a pole to gain more height

bounce   bound   hop   leap   spring

420   junk   n.

*cast-offs   dregs   garbage   leavings
left-overs   odds and ends   refuse
rejects   remnants   rubbish   scraps
second-hand goods   trash   waste*

421   just   adj.

fair

disinterested   acting fairly because not influenced by personal advantage
impartial   unprejudiced; unbiased
neutral   without any feelings on either side of a question
objective   not influenced by personal feelings
open-minded   receptive to new ideas
unprejudiced   fair in judgement
upright   strictly honourable

422   keep   v.

fulfil   carry out
maintain   keep in good condition
manage   have under effective control
preserve   keep safe; keep in an unchanged condition
store   put away for future use

hold on to   stock

423   kill   v.

assassinate   kill an important person by violent means
execute   put a condemned person to death
hang   kill by suspending from a rope that tightens round the neck
liquidate   get rid of, especially by killing
murder   kill a person unlawfully and on purpose
remove   do away with

silence force to stop expressing opinions or making opposing statements, usually by killing

*bump off   knock off   polish off
slay   snuff out*

424   kind   n.

sort   type

genre particular style of art or literature
genus group of animals or plants with common characteristics, usually containing several species
order group of plants or animals classified as similar in many ways
species group of plants or animals alike in all important ways, and able to breed together
variety type which is different from others in the group to which it belongs

breed   clan   kin   stock   tribe

425   king   n.

crowned head   monarch   sovereign

potentate ruler with direct power over his people
supreme head highest in authority or rank

majesty   ruler

426   knife   n.

bayonet long knife fixed to the end of a rifle
bowie knife strong hunting knife with short hilt and a guard for the hand
cutlass short, heavy sword with a slightly curved blade
jack-knife large folding pocket knife
machete broad heavy-bladed knife used in Central America as a tool and weapon

rapier long, light, thin double-edged sword with sharp point
sabre cavalry sword with a curved blade
scimitar short, curved oriental sword
stiletto small dagger with a slender, tapered blade
switchblade weapon with a blade that springs out when a button is pressed; flick-knife
tomahawk fighting axe of North American Indians

dagger   dirk

427   know   v. (i)

comprehend grasp mentally
fathom get at the true meaning of
grasp succeed in understanding
understand perceive the meaning of

*appreciate   be aware of
be conscious of   be familiar with
feel certain   have in one's head*

know   v. (ii)

recognize know again; identify from one's previous knowledge or experience

428   knowledge   n.

education systematic instruction designed to give knowledge and develop skill
erudition great learning
data facts as information
instruction process of teaching; advice on how to do something
learning deep knowledge gained by study
scholarship great learning in a particular academic subject
schooling being taught in a school; training of an animal

429 land n.

cape high land jutting out into the sea

continent one of the seven main land masses of the earth

country nation or state; the land it occupies

ground earth or soil; surface of the earth

homeland country of one's birth or where one lives

isthmus narrow area of land with sea on each side joining two land masses

mainland country or continent without its adjacent islands

peninsula piece of land projecting far into the sea that is almost surrounded by water

terrain stretch of land, with regard to its natural features

mother country   *native land*
terra firma

430 lasting adj.

enduring

immortal living or continuing for ever; famous for all time

imperishable which will not wear out or decay

indestructible incapable of being broken up; very long-lasting

persisting continuing, especially past expected time

long-lived   *never-ending*   *unending*

431 lastly adv.

finally   in conclusion

hindmost   *in last place*   *rearmost*

432 late adj.

behind time

overdue left unpaid too long; later than expected

tardy slow or late to act, move, or happen

unpunctual not arriving or doing things at the appointed time

behind schedule

433 lately adv.

a little while back   a short time ago
not long before   of late
recently

434 laugh v.

chuckle laugh softly or to oneself

giggle laugh in a silly or nervous way

guffaw laugh crudely and noisily

roar laugh long and loudly

shriek laugh shrilly

snigger giggle in a disrespectful, sly way

titter snigger in a disrespectful, very quiet way

cackle   *chortle*   *split one's sides*

435 lazy adj.

idle   indolent   slothful

lethargic extremely lacking in energy

shiftless lacking in purpose, ability, or effort

slack not properly careful or quick

sluggish slow-moving; not alert or active

unambitious without desire for success, power, or riches

unenterprising lacking in initiative and readiness to undertake or experiment

unindustrious lacking the will to work hard

easy-going

436 lest conj.

for fear that   in case
so as to avoid the risk of

437 let v. (i)

allow   permit

assent to   agree to
authorize   give power to or
  permission for
empower   give someone the power or
  lawful right
sanction   accept, approve, or permit

allow to pass

438 let v. (ii)

lease   rent

charter   let or hire a ship, aircraft, or
  vehicle
contract   arrange or undertake by
  formal agreement
hire out   allow the temporary use for
  payment
lend   allow someone the use of
  something for a time without
  payment
sublet   let accommodation that one is
  renting oneself

439 liar n.

fibber   prevaricator

false witness   person who gives false
  evidence in a law court
libeller   person who publishes a false
  statement about another
perjurer   person who deliberately
  gives false evidence while on oath

story-teller

440 lie v. (i)

laze   spend time in idle relaxation
loll   stand, sit, lean, or rest in a lazy,
  loose position

recline   lean backwards; lie down
repose   lie still and comfortably at rest
sprawl   stretch oneself out slackly and
  awkwardly

relax

lie v. (ii)

fib   prevaricate; speak untruthfully

441 lift v.

elevate   raise

brandish   wave a thing in display or
  threateningly
hoist   raise or haul up; lift with ropes
  and pulleys
lever   move or force open by a bar
  pivoted on a fixed point
uphold   support; keep from falling

raise aloft   *raise high*

442 like v.

be fond of

delight in   take great pleasure in
enjoy   get happiness from
fancy   wish for; have a liking for
feel inclined   have a willingness to
relish   enjoy greatly

take pleasure in

443 likely adj.

probable

conceivable   able to be imagined or
  believed
imaginable   able to be pictured in the
  mind
promising   likely to turn out well or
  produce good results

444 likeness n.

resemblance   similarity

copy thing made to look like another
facsimile reproduction of a
  document, book or painting
reproduction copy of a painting, or
  piece of furniture, made in imitation
  of an earlier style

445 liking n.

favouritism unfairly generous
  treatment
fondness having a gentle and tender
  liking for
penchant strong leaning towards
preference desire for one thing rather
  than another
taste personal liking

attachment   attraction   regard

446 list n.

catalogue list of items, usually in a
  special order and with a description
  of each
directory book containing names,
  addresses, and telephone numbers of
  individuals or firms
index alphabetical list at the back of a
  book of the main names and subjects
  in it, and the pages where they can
  be found
inventory detailed list of goods or
  furniture
line-up row of people or things got
  together for a particular purpose
register official list of names, items,
  or attendances
roll official list or register, especially
  with names
roster list showing people's turns of
  duty

447 little adj.

small

diminutive remarkably small
petite small, dainty build applied to a
  woman
stunted not properly or fully-grown
tiny very small

*bantam   dwarfish   light-weight
midget   pigmy*

448 liveable adj.

bearable able to be put up with
habitable suitable for living in;
  inhabitable
occupiable able to be lived in for the
  time but without comfort

449 lively adj.

full of life

animated full of spirit and excitement
brisk quick and active in movement
frisky playful

enthusiastic

450 load n.

*boatload   burden   cargo   contents
freight   lorryload   merchandise
shipload   waggonload*

451 lonely adj. (i)

estranged cold and unfriendly
outcast driven out or rejected
solitary alone, without companions;
  fond of being alone

*alone   companionless   friendless
unwanted*

452 lonely adj. (ii)

*deserted   remote   unfrequented
uninhabited*

453 look v.

behold see; observe
glance give a quick, brief look
glimpse catch a brief view of
glower stare hard and sullenly
leer give a sideways, sneering, or
  suggestive look or grin
peep look through a narrow opening,
  or from a concealed place
peer look searchingly or with
  difficulty
regard look upon in a particular way
scowl make an angry or threatening
  frown

454 look for v (i)

cast around for hunt for
search for seek

455 look for v. (ii)

anticipate regard as likely; foresee
expect believe that something will
  happen
reckon on count or depend on

456 loose adj.

*detached slack unattached
unchained unclasped unconnected
unfastened unfettered unhooked
unrestrained untied*

457 lot n.

*considerable number good deal
heap large quantity load mass
pile stack tons*

458 love v.

adore love deeply; worship as divine
adulate flatter or praise excessively
be infatuated with be filled
  temporarily with an intense,
  unreasoning love for a person or
  thing

care for feel affection for
cherish look after lovingly
crave for long for intensely
desire want very much
have a crush on have a strong,
  foolish and short-lived liking or
  love for someone
hold dear regard highly and with
  reverence
idolize feel excessive admiration or
  devotion
lust for strong or excessive desire,
  especially sexual
pine for feel great longing for
  something, usually unattainable
worship honour or adore as a god
yearn for have a strong, loving, and
  sad desire for

think the world of treasure

459 lovely adj.

attractive pleasing in appearance or
  effect
beautiful giving great pleasure to the
  senses
becoming looking very well on the
  wearer
charming arousing liking or
  admiration
comely good-looking
delightful giving great pleasure
glamorous romantically fascinating
pretty pleasing or appealing in a
  delicate or graceful way

*alluring enchanting fascinating
good-looking ravishing seductive
sexy*

460 luckily adv.

by good fortune fortunately
happily

461 **lure** v.

attract get the attention of
decoy deceive a person or animal
  into danger
entice attract or persuade by offering
  something pleasant
inveigle trick someone into doing
  something
tempt arouse a desire

ensnare

462 **mad** adj.

angry irate

enraged very angry
frantic wildly excited or agitated by
  anxiety
fuming seething with anger
furious violently angry
indignant angry because of
  something unjust or wicked
infuriated intensely angry
irritated impatient or slightly angry
  at small things
nettled stung by unkind or
  thoughtless remarks or actions
raging violently and noisily angry
riled stirred up and agitated
vexed worried and annoyed

cross *peeved* *peevish* *raving*

463 **magnificent** adj.

awe-inspiring filling with respect,
  fear and wonder
glorious having, or worthy of, great
  fame, honour, or beauty
luxurious very fine, costly, and
  extremely comfortable
majestic stately and dignified;
  imposing
noble possessing excellent qualities,
  especially in one's character; free
  from pettiness, or meanness
regal like or fit for a king

sublime of the very highest or most
  impressive kind
sumptuous expensive or extravagant

gorgeous *grand* *great* *splendid*
superb

464 **main** adj.

chief principal

crucial of deciding importance
paramount supreme
predominant greater than others in
  power, influence, number or intensity
primary of the first importance

465 **mainly** adv.

chiefly mostly principally

by and large *especially*
for the most part *on the whole*
primarily

466 **make** v.

assemble gather or put together
build make by putting parts or
  materials together
construct make by putting together
  or combining parts
devise think out, plan, or invent
draw up prepare a draft, usually of a
  legal document
erect set up or build
manufacture produce on a large scale
  by machinery
produce make or bring into existence
  from materials, labour, or thought

467 **manner** n.

custom usual way of behaving or
  doing something
method way of doing something
mode way in which a thing is done;
  current fashion

technique   method in which a skilled
  activity is carried out
style   manner of writing, speaking, or
  doing something
system   ordered set of ideas, methods,
  or ways of working

468   many   adj.

numerous

innumerable   too many to be counted
multitudinous   very large in number
sundry   a few; varying
various   more than one; individual
  and separate

469   map   n.

atlas   book of maps
chart   map designed for navigators on
  water or in the air
gazeteer   book or section of book that
  lists and describes places
graph   diagram showing the
  relationship between two sets of
  quantities
grid   network of squares on maps,
  numbered for reference
plan   map of a town or district
projection   representation of the
  surface of the earth on a plane surface
relief map   map showing hills and
  valleys either by shading or
  moulding
topographical map   map showing
  details of the surface features of
  a region

470   marvellous   adj.

astounding   breathtaking   extraordinary   miraculous   remarkable
unheard-of   unparalleled
unprecedented

471   mature   adj.
fully developed   full-grown

adult   full-grown person or animal
full-blown   developed to its fullest
  and best extent
ripe   ready to be gathered and used
seasoned   brought into a fit condition
  for use by drying, treating, or
  allowing to ripen

ready

472   maybe   adv.
perhaps

as the case may be   for all I know
possibly

473   mean   adj. (i)

catchpenny   worthless, but appearing
  attractive through cheapness or
  showiness
cheap   low in price; good value
inferior   not good or less good in
  quality or value
low-grade   low in quality or standard
meretricious   attractive on the
  surface, but of no value or
  importance
shabby   appearing poor because of
  wear
shoddy   made or done cheaply and
  badly
tatty   untidy and uncared for
tawdry   cheaply showy, but without
  real value
worthless   not worth anything;
  useless

474   mean   adj. (ii)
ungenerous

grudging   resenting having to give or
  allow something
miserly   hoarding money and
  spending as little as possible
narrow-minded   considering only

part of a question or favouring only
one opinion
petty having a limited, ungenerous
mind
small-minded narrow or selfish in
outlook

mean-spirited

475 **meek** adj.

humble

forbearing patient and long-suffering
lowly simple and plain in manner
unprotesting accepting things
without complaint

476 **meet** v.

accost go up and speak to, especially
boldly
chance upon come upon by chance
encounter meet unexpectedly
face meet or oppose firmly and not
try to avoid
respond to speak or act in answer to

face up to make the acquaintance of
run across

477 **meeting** n.

assembly people meeting for a special
purpose
conference meeting for discussion
and exchange of opinions
congregation group of people
worshipping together
congress formal meeting of a group
of people with a shared purpose
convention large formal meeting of a
group with common interests
reception formal party held to
receive guests
rendezvous arrangement to meet, or
the place chosen to meet
tryst appointment to meet secretly

gathering get-together

478 **mend** v.

repair

remedy put or make right
restore bring back to its original state
by repairing or rebuilding

fix up *patch up* *put back together*
put right

479 **merely** adj. & adv.

just *nothing more than* *only*
simply *solely*

480 **messy** adj.

untidy

chaotic in a state of complete
disorder and confusion
dishevelled ruffled and untidy in
appearance
filthy disgustingly dirty
frowsy shabby and untidy
slovenly unclean and untidy in
appearance
unkempt looking neglected

frumpy *sloppy*

481 **mind** n.

common sense practical good sense
and judgement
consciousness awareness of one's self
and surroundings
intellect mind's power to reason and
acquire knowledge
intelligence ability to reason
mentality one's characteristic attitude
of mind; outlook
sanity soundness of mind; freedom
from lasting mental disturbance

brain-power

482 **miser** n.

scrooge *skinflint*

483 miserly adj.

niggardly unwilling to spend money
parsimonious extremely careful or
  reluctant in spending
stingy grudging in spending and
  giving
tight-fisted mean with money and
  possessions

cheese-paring frugal money-grubbing penny-pinching

484 mist n.

fog thick mist that is difficult to see
  through
haze light mist or smoke
smog fog polluted by smoke and
  chemical fumes
vapour particles of moisture or other
  substance suspended in air and visible
  as clouds or smoke

485 mistake n.

error

blunder mistake made especially
  through ignorance or carelessness
boob stupid embarrassing mistake
fallacy false idea or belief
faux pas embarrassing social mistake
  or indiscretion
gaffe tactless remark
inaccuracy error or slip in fact or
  calculation
miscalculation incorrect estimate
misunderstanding failure to
  understand correctly
oversight unintended failure to notice
  or do something

486 modern adj.

up-to-date

avant-garde producing or using an
  ultra-modern style, especially in art
  or literature

contemporary belonging to the same
  period, present or past
novel new, especially clever or
  unfamiliar
topical related to, dealing with, or
  being a subject of present interest

*experimental present-day
the latest thing*

487 modest adj.

unassuming

humble having or showing a low
  opinion of one's own importance
self-effacing avoiding the attention of
  others
unpretentious not showy or
  pompous

488 mountain n.

alp mountain peak; pasture-land on
  mountains in Switzerland
butte isolated, steep-sided, flat-
  topped hill
chain number of connected
  mountains
escarpment long, continuous steep
  face of a ridge or plateau
highlands mountainous country
peak pointed top, especially of a
  mountain
precipice very steep or vertical face
  of a cliff or rock
range connected line of mountains or
  hills
sierra low range or area of sharply-
  pointed mountains in Spain or
  Spanish America
summit top, especially the highest
  part on the top of a mountain

489 much adj.

a great deal

abundant more than enough

ample quite enough
bountiful given generously
considerable fairly large in amount or size
plentiful in large quantities or numbers

490 **muddled** adj.

confused disordered

botched spoilt by poor or clumsy work
bungled tackled clumsily and without success
disarranged out of order or position
disorderly lacking order and tidiness
disorganized lacking orderly system
jumbled mixed in a confused way
snarled jammed and difficult to free
tangled twisted into a confused mass

491 **muddy** adj.

miry deeply and stickily muddy
mucky very dirty and messy
sludgy greasy and muddy
slushy covered in partly-melted and often muddy snow

boggy *marshy* *swampy*

492 **must** v.

be compelled to be forced to
be obliged to have a duty to; bound to do
have to be obliged to
ought to have a duty to; be advised to

493 **nag** v.

badger annoy with frequent requests or questions
carp keep finding unnecessary fault

grumble complain in a bad-tempered way
hector torment by teasing
bully

494 **naked** adj.

nude

stark-naked completely without clothes

in one's birthday suit *in the altogether*
in the raw *unclothed* *undressed*
without a stitch on

495 **name** v.

address speak to; refer to in speaking; deliver a speech to
appoint put in or choose for a position, job, or purpose
baptize give a name to at a Christian ceremony
call name; describe or address as
christen give a Christian name to in baptism; give a nickname to
entitle give a name to a book, poem, or picture
identify recognize as being a particular person or thing
mention speak or write about briefly; refer to by name
nominate suggest or appoint someone to a position
specify refer to exactly

496 **nameless** adj.

anonymous

obscure not at all well-known; unimportant
undesignated without a special name or description
unidentified not recognized as being a certain person or thing
unknown not known to anyone
unspecified referred to but not described

497 namely adv.

as a case in point   for instance
specifically   that is   that is to say

498 nasty adj. (i)

disgusting   very unpleasant; against
  one's principles
indecent   offending against what is
  fitting and proper
objectionable   causing disapproval
obnoxious   extremely unpleasant
unsavoury   morally unpleasant or
  unacceptable

blasphemous   foul mouthed
revolting   sickening

499 nasty adj. (ii)
unkind   unpleasant

despicable   deserving to be despised
ill-natured   bad-tempered and unkind
malicious   wishing or intending to
  hurt others
spiteful   desiring to annoy or hurt in
  small ways
surly   bad-tempered and unfriendly
vicious   wicked or violently cruel

500 nature n.

character   qualities that make a
  person or thing different from others
disposition   person's usual frame of
  mind; temperament
personality   distinctive qualities of a
  person
temperament   person's nature as it
  controls the way he behaves, feels and
  thinks

make-up

501 naughty adj. (i)

defiant   fearlessly refusing to obey
delinquent   breaking the law or doing
  socially unacceptable things
disobedient   failing or refusing to
  obey
exasperating   annoying greatly
impish   annoying in a harmless way
mischievous   teasing or annoying
  playfully
reprehensible   deserving to be told off
  or blamed
roguish   playfully naughty in a
  deliberate and affected way

undisciplined   unruly   wayward

502 naughty adj. (ii)
improper

risqué   slightly indecent
smutty   morally improper
titillating   pleasantly exciting or
  stimulating

503 nearly adv.
almost

all but   just about   more or less
not quite   roughly

504 neglect v.

abstain from   keep oneself from doing
disregard   pay no attention to; treat
  as of no importance
ignore   take no notice of; pretend not
  to know or see
overlook   fail to observe or consider
shun   keep away from
spurn   reject scornfully

505 nevertheless adv. & conj.
however   in any case   in spite of
none the less   not withstanding

506 newspaper n.

daily newspaper sold every day
 except Sunday and perhaps Saturday
tabloid newspaper with a small page
 size
weekly newspaper or magazine
 appearing once a week

507 next adj. (i)

adjacent adjoining bordering

next adj. (ii)

*after ensuing following
subsequent*

508 nice adj.

agreeable pleasant pleasing

amusing causing smiles or laughter
attractive pleasing in appearance or
 effect
delightful highly pleasing
enjoyable giving pleasure
friendly kindly and helpful

*amiable charitable cheering
congenial generous kindly
likeable satisfactory sympathetic
understanding warm-hearted*

509 noise n.

bedlam wild, noisy place or activity;
 madhouse
clamour loud, continuous, confused
 noise, especially of shouting
clang loud, ringing sound
din loud echoing and annoying noise
hubbub loud, confused noise of
 voices
hullaballoo loud, confused noise of
 voices protesting
pandemonium wild and noisy
 confusion

racket noisy disturbance
uproar outburst of noise from
 excitement or anger

jangle jingle rattle

510 none pron.

*no-one no part not a bit not any
not one*

511 nonsense n.

absurdity funny or foolish thing
 because clearly unsuitable
claptrap worthless talk or ideas used
 only to win applause
drivel silly and meaningless talk
gibberish meaningless sounds
gobbledegook pompous language
 used by officials
ridiculousness talk or actions
 deserving to be laughed at
stupidity sayings or actions lacking
 in common sense

*balderdash craziness
stuff and nonsense tommyrot*

512 note v.

record write down

annotate add short notes of
 explanation
catalogue make a list of places,
 names, or goods in a special order
chronicle record historical events in
 the order they happened
enter put details in a list or book
insert put extra detail between lines
 already written
register put into an official record

513 notorious adj.

of ill repute

disreputable having a bad reputation

infamous being widely known for wicked behaviour

stigmatized branded as something shameful

514 now adv.

at present immediately
straight away

515 object v.

demur show signs of being against something
disapprove have or express an unfavourable opinion
dissent have or express a different opinion
expostulate make a friendly protest; reason or argue with a person
oppose argue or fight against
protest express annoyance or disagreement
remonstrate argue in protest

516 obsolete adj.

antiquated old and not suited to present needs or conditions
discontinued no longer made or offered for sale
outdated no longer in general use
outmoded no longer in fashion
redundant surplus to requirements; no longer needed for any available job

517 obvious adj.

evident manifest

explicit clear and fully expressed
palpable easily perceived by the senses; easily understood
patent easy to see; unconcealed
recognizable knowable from one's previous knowledge or experience

clear as crystal clear-cut
plain as a pikestaff

518 odd adj.

strange unusual

abnormal different from what is ordinary or expected
eccentric different from the usual in behaviour and dress; odd
grotesque very odd or unnatural
incongruous comparing strangely with what surrounds it
queer differing from the normal in a strange way
unconventional not following the accepted customs, especially in an original way
unorthodox not generally or officially accepted

bizarre capricious idiosyncratic
peculiar

519 offend v.

affront be rude to or hurt the feelings of, especially in public
disgust cause a very strong feeling of dislike and/or indignation
humiliate cause to feel disgraced
insult treat with scorn and abuse
provoke make angry; rouse to action
repulse refuse coldly

520 official adj.

authorized granted official permission
authoritative recognized as being true or reliable
certified declared formally as being correct
lawful permitted by law
legitimate in accordance with the law, or with certain rules or standards
sanctioned formally accepted or approved

accredited approved governmental
legal licensed

521 officious adj.

inquisitive excessively curious, especially about the affairs of others; eager to learn
interfering pushing oneself into someone else's affairs
meddlesome often interfering in people's affairs
prying finding out secretly about someone else's private affairs

bossy   nosey

522 often adv.

frequently

generally as a rule; commonly
habitually regularly out of habit
periodically at regular intervals
usually normally; on most occasions

repeatedly

523 once adv. & conj.

on one occasion

formerly in earlier times
previously coming before in time or order

524 opinion n.

assessment estimate of the worth, quality or likelihood of
assumption something taken as a fact without proof
attitude manner of thinking, feeling, or behaving
belief feeling that something is true or real
conviction firm opinion or belief
feeling idea or belief not wholly based on reason
impression effect produced on the mind; uncertain idea, belief or remembrance
judgement ability to use good sense

to achieve a balanced view point
observation comment or remark
stance way of thinking; mental attitude
standpoint position from which things are seen and opinions formed
view personal opinion about something

525 order n. (i)

command

dictate order which should be obeyed
directive general instruction issued by authority
instructions statements making known to a person what he is required to do; directions
regulation official rule
request something asked for, especially politely

526 order n. (ii)

sequence

grouping planned arrangement of things within units
harmony agreement in action, opinion, or feeling
symmetry similarity or balance between the parts of something
tidiness neat and orderly arrangement
uniformity state in which everything is unvarying

orderliness

527 ordinary adj.

common   normal

commonplace well-known and lacking originality
conventional following accepted practices and customs too closely
familiar well-known; usual

prevailing most common or general
typical combining and showing the
  main signs of a particular kind,
  group, or class

common-or-garden *everyday*
run-of-the-mill

528 **pain** n.

ache dull, continuous pain
agony extreme mental or physical
  suffering
anguish extreme misery or grief
colic severe pain in the stomach and
  bowels
discomfort not being easy in body or
  mind
pang sudden, sharp feeling of pain in
  body or mind
soreness tenderness of a wound,
  injury, or muscle
stitch sudden, sharp pain in the
  muscles at the side of the body
suffering general pain, misery, or
  grief
twinge sudden, brief, darting, or
  stabbing pain

heartache

529 **pale** adj.

anaemic pale and sickly-looking;
  lacking vigour and vitality
ashen drained of colour; pale grey
  colour of ashes
blanched colourless; whitened
bleached whitened by sunlight or
  chemicals
pallid unusually pale, especially from
  illness
pasty unhealthily pale
sallow of an unhealthy yellowish
  colour
wan unnaturally pale, especially
  from grief or sickness
washed-out very tired and faded-
  looking

waxen like wax in paleness or
  smoothness

bloodless *deathlike* *ghastly*
ghostly

530 **paper** n.

charter official document granting
  rights and freedoms
deed paper that proves and records
  an agreement
diploma document awarding a
  qualification, recording examination
  success, or completing a course of
  study
document paper giving information
  or evidence about something
newsprint cheap kind of paper used
  mostly for newspapers
parchment heavy paper-like material
  made from animal skins
stationery any writing materials
title document conferring the legal
  right to ownership
warrant written order signed by an
  official of the law
will written directions made by a
  person for the disposal of property
  and money after death

certificate *licence* *testament*

531 **parent** n.
father mother

ancestor person, especially one living
  a long time ago, from whom another
  is descended
forbear person from whom the stated
  person is descended
foster-parents persons who take care
  of and bring up a child as their own
godparents persons who undertake
  to see that a child is brought up as
  a Christian
guardian person who legally agrees
  to look after another's child,
  especially after the parent's death

sire   old word for father

step-parent   person whom one's
father or mother has remarried

532   **part**   n.

complement   something that
completes another; number or
quantity needed to fill something
division   part of the whole which has
been divided
element   one of the parts that make up
a whole
fraction   very small part, piece, or
amount
ingredient   a particular one of a
mixture of things, especially in
cooking
majority   greatest number or part of a
group or class
minority   smallest number or part of a
group or class
portion   share or part of something
remnant   small remaining quantity,
part, or number of people or things
section   distinct part or portion of
something
segment   any of the parts into which
something may be cut or divided
slice   thin, flat piece cut from
something
snippet   small scrap or fragment,
especially of something spoken or
written

chunk   hunk   particle   wedge

533   **parting**   n. (i)

dissociation   declaration that one has
no connection with something
divorce   separation, especially one
which is total
rift   break in friendly relations
between people, or in the unity of a
group
separation   breaking, coming or being
apart

534   **parting**   n. (ii)

departure   farewell   leave-taking

535   **passable**   adj.

acceptable

adequate   enough or suitable for the
purpose
admissible   able or deserving to be
considered or allowed
allowable   may be permitted
presentable   fit to be seen, shown, or
heard in public
tolerable   fairly good; able to be put
up with

middling   so-so

536   **passive**   adj.

inactive

apathetic   lacking feeling, interest, or
desire to act
inert   very slow to move or take
action
non-participating   not willing to take
part or share in an activity
stolid   showing little or no emotion or
interest
submissive   willing to obey humbly
and without question
undemonstrative   not expressing one's
feelings openly
unresisting   not opposing or fighting
against
unresponsive   not reacting warmly by
words or feelings

537   **pathetic**   adj.

heart-rending   very distressing;
causing great sorrow
lamentable   wretched, regrettable, or
distressing
paltry   worthless, trivial,
contemptible
touching   rousing kindly feelings,
sympathy, or pity

538 patience n

diligence steady and attentive hard work

doggedness refusal to give up in the face of difficulty

endurance ability to withstand pain, hardship, or strain

forbearance control of one's feelings, showing patience and tolerance

perseverance ability to go on steadfastly, especially in something difficult or tedious

restraint self-control

self-possession calm and dignified control over one's own feelings and actions

539 pay v.

advance lend money or pay it before the proper time

compensate make a suitable payment in return for loss or damage

disburse pay out money

indemnify compensate for loss, injury, or expense

refund give back money, especially for an unsatisfactory article

remunerate reward or pay a person for services rendered

foot the bill

540 people n.

human beings

clan group of families, all originally descended from one family

clientele those who use the services of professional people, businesses, or shops

community group with common interests or origins

humankind human beings

kinsmen blood relations, or relations by marriage

mankind human race

mortals people (subject to death)

nation large community of people of mainly common descent, living in one territory under one government

persons individual human beings without regard to sex

population total inhabitants of a place, district, or country

public members of the community in general or a particular section of it

race one of the great divisions of mankind with certain inherited physical characteristics in common

residents people who live permanently in a place

society large group of people with shared language, customs and laws

folk

541 perfect adj.

faultless ideal

admirable worthy of being respected and looked up to

excellent extremely good; of the highest quality

exemplary suitable to be copied; serving as a warning

incomparable above comparison; matchless; unequalled

unblemished free from flaws or defects; spotlessly clean

542 perhaps adv.

maybe possibly

there is a chance that

543 persuade v.

convince

convert cause a person to change his attitude or beliefs, usually concerning religion

enlist secure as a means of support

induce lead someone to act, usually by persuasion

influence   have an effect on someone's character, beliefs, or actions
prevail upon   succeed in persuading or inducing

win over

544   **petty**   adj.

trifling   trivial   unimportant

insignificant   having little or no importance, value, or influence
minor   lesser or secondary in amount, extent, importance, or degree

inessential

545   **picture**   v.

imagine

visualize   form a picture of someone or something in the mind

546   **picture**   n.

collage   artistic composition made by sticking various materials or objects on to a surface
description   account intended to give mental image
engraving   print made from cuts on wood, stone, or metal
etching   picture printed from a metal plate cut with acids
fresco   watercolour picture painted on a wall or ceiling before the plaster is dry
old master   great painter of former times, or one of his pictures
portrait   painting, drawing, or photograph of a real person
representation   artistic likeness or image
still life   painting of lifeless things, such as cut flowers or fruit

sketch   *snapshot*

547   **pink**   adj.

rose

salmon-pink

548   **pitiful**   adj.

pitiable

abject   as low as possible; not deserving respect
beggarly   mean and insufficient; very poor
wretched   poor, miserable, unhappy

549   **plan**   n.

arrangement   agreed preparations for doing something
plot   secret plan by several people to do harm
procedure   set of actions necessary for doing something
programme   definite plan of what is to be done
scheme   clever, sometimes dishonest, plan; orderly planned arrangement
strategy   particular plan for winning success in a particular activity, especially military
tactic   device calculated to achieve a desired result

proposal

550   **pleasant**   adj.

agreeable   pleasing

affable   easy to talk to; polite and friendly
delectable   enjoyable; especially pleasing to the taste
delightful   giving great pleasure
enjoyable   receiving pleasure from
gratifying   satisfying pleasurably

551 pleasure n.

enjoyment

contentment happy and satisfied
  with what one has
exhilaration enlivening happiness
fulfilment deep satisfaction of a need
glee triumphant merriment
gratification act or state of being
  pleasurably satisfied
rejoicing gladness or great joy,
  celebrating some event

gladness   happiness

552 plight n.

crisis time of acute difficulty or
  danger
dilemma situation in which one must
  chose between two evils
extremity highest degree of need,
  suffering, misfortune, or danger
predicament difficult, perplexing, or
  unpleasant situation
quandary state of perplexity and
  doubt

scrape

553 pointless adj.

meaningless   purposeless

fatuous foolishly self-satisfied
immaterial of no importance
irrelevant not having any connection
  with something
vain without result; useless

absurd

554 poor adj.

destitute lacking the simplest
  necessary things of life
impecunious having little or no
  money
impoverished made poor

penurious lacking money or means;
  mean with money

badly-off   down-and-out   needy
penniless   poverty-stricken

555 possible adj.

conceivable able to be imagined or
  believed
credible worthy of belief
feasible able to be carried out
practicable able to be successfully
  used or acted upon
probable likely to happen or be true

attainable

556 practice n.

convention accepted way of social
  behaviour
custom usual way of behaving or
  doing something
habit something done frequently and
  almost without thinking
procedure way or order of directing
  business or accomplishing something
routine regular, ordinary way of
  doing things
rule customary or normal state of
  things or course of action

observance

557 practised adj.

experienced

knowledgeable well-informed
seasoned experienced through
  training and practice
versed possessing a thorough
  knowledge or skill

adroit   dextrous   expert   masterful

558 **predict** v.

forecast tell in advance what is likely
to happen
foresee be aware of or realize a thing
beforehand
prophesy foretell future events as if
by divine inspiration

559 **pretty** adj.

appealing pleasing and interesting
attractive having good looks
beautiful giving great pleasure to the
senses or the mind
captivating exciting and capturing
the fancy
dainty small and delicately pretty
elegant graceful, refined, and
dignified in style or appearance
enchanting filling with intense delight
good-looking having a pleasing
appearance
gorgeous strikingly beautiful or
magnificent
graceful very pleasing in movement,
form, or behaviour
handsome fine-looking and well-
proportioned
lovely attractive to both heart and
eye
stunning extremely attractive;
splendid

*engaging exquisite fascinating
ornamental picturesque stylish
winsome*

560 **price** n.

charge cost

duty tax charged on certain goods or
on imports
estimate rough calculation of the cost
of doing something
expense spending of money; amount
of money spent

fare price charged for a passenger to
travel
fee sum payable to a professional
person for advice or services
hire use of a thing for a time for
payment
levy payment imposed or collected
by authority or by force
penalty fine or forfeit imposed as a
punishment
quotation price of something as
known at that time
rent money paid regularly for the use
of property or an object
retail price price of goods sold to
customers for their own use, not for
resale
tariff list of fixed charges, especially
for rooms and meals at a hotel
toll tax or duty paid for the use of a
public road, bridge, or harbour
wholesale price price of goods sold in
large quantities for resale

forfeit valuation

561 **pride** n.

arrogance exaggerated and self-
important pride
bumptiousness offensive and self-
assertive conceit
conceit too high an opinion of one's
own abilities and value
haughtiness high and mighty
manner; looking down on others
vanity far too proud of one's
appearance, possessions, or
achievements

*complacence presumption self-
importance self-satisfaction*

562 **prisoner** n.

captive person or animal taken
prisoner and/or unable to escape

convict   person found guilty of a
crime and sent to prison
jailbird   person who has spent a lot of
time in prison
trusty   prisoner who is granted special
privileges because of continous good
behaviour

563   private   adj.

confidential   trusted with private
matters; to be kept secret
off-the-record   not to be written down
in the notes of the meeting
restricted   limited to selected persons
unofficial   not yet said to be true by
those in charge

564   prize   n. (i)

award   something that is given,
especially on the basis of merit or need
jackpot   largest amount of money to
be won in a game of chance
lottery   arrangement in which people
buy tickets, a few of which are picked
by chance to win prizes
sweepstake   form of betting in which
the winners gain all the money paid in
trophy   object given as a prize or
token of victory
windfall   unexpectedly lucky gift or
good fortune

winnings

565   prize   n. (ii)

booty   goods stolen by thieves or
taken by a victorious army
loot   goods stolen, as in wartime or
during riots
plunder   valuables, goods, or sacred
items taken by force
seizure   goods taken forcibly
spoils   anything of value seized by
violence, especially in war

566   probably   adv.

likely

apparently   doubtless
in all likelihood

567   procession   n.

cavalcade   procession of people on
horseback, in carriages, and in cars
column   long narrow formation of
troops, people, or vehicles
cortège   funeral procession or
procession of attendants
file   line of people or things one
behind the other
march past   ceremonial march past a
saluting-point
motorcade   procession of cars
parade   formal assembly of troops for
inspection; procession of people or
things, especially in a display or
exhibition
retinue   number of attendants
accompanying an important person
train   number of people or animals
moving in a line

march

568   profit   n.

gain

advantage   more favourable position;
benefit or profit
benefit   something helpful,
favourable, or profitable
income   money received regularly for
work, or as interest
interest   money paid for the use of
money lent
return   money gained from an
investment, transaction, or venture
revenue   annual amount of money
received by a country from taxes
yield   amount produced; quantity
obtained

recompense

569 promptly adv.

punctually

briskly doing what is required without undue delay
expediently suitable to the circumstances
timely happening or coming at just the right moment

immediately *unhesitatingly*

570 proof n.

confirmation act of establishing proof of the truth of something
corroboration supporting or strengthening fact or opinion by fresh information
evidence anything that establishes a fact, or gives reason for believing something
ratification formal approval or consent
validation declaration of legal acceptability

documentation

571 proper adj.

correct fitting

becoming suitable
decent conforming to the accepted standards of what is respectable
decorous correct in manners and behaviour
seemly in accordance with accepted standards of good taste

572 proud adj.

arrogant too proud and self-important
cocksure too sure of oneself
conceited valuing oneself too highly
haughty disdainful; having or showing arrogance

patronizing treating others as less important or of less worth than oneself
self-assertive pushing forward one's own abilities or claims
self-important having too high an opinion of one's own importance
supercilious scornful and high and mighty in manner

big-headed *condescending*
disdainful *pompous* *snobbish*

573 proverb n.

adage traditional saying accepted by many as true
aphorism short wise saying
axiom accepted general truth or principle
epigram short witty saying or poem
maxim rule for good and sensible behaviour
platitude commonplace remark, especially one uttered solemnly as if it were new
truism statement of something that is obviously or indisputably true

574 pull v.

drag pull along the ground with effort or difficulty
draw pull a cart or sledge
tow pull along behind by a rope or chain
tug pull suddenly and strongly
yank make a sudden, sharp pull

575 pure adj.

immaculate without spot or stain
unalloyed not weakened or spoiled, especially by unpleasant feelings
uncontaminated not mixed with dirty or poisonous matter

chaste *stainless* *wholesome*

576 push v.

impel send, drive, or push forward
jog shake slightly with a jerk or push
jolt dislodge or shake with a sudden
  jerk
jostle knock or push roughly,
  especially when in a crowd
nudge push slightly or gradually
poke push sharply with the end of a
  finger or stick
propel drive or cause to move
  forward
shove push roughly
trundle roll along; move along
  heavily on a wheel or wheels

press forward *shoulder through*
squeeze through

577 put v.

place

deposit set down carefully or in its
  proper place
drop fall by force of gravity from not
  being held
lay place or put on a surface or in a
  certain position
locate fix or set in a certain place
plant set in place; put seeds or plants
  in the ground
plonk place or drop down with a
  hollow sound
pose sit, stand, or be put in a
  particular position
position put in a suitable place for a
  particular purpose
situate allot a site to
station place or stand in a position
  already decided

park

578 puzzle n.

conundrum puzzling question or
  problem

enigma person, thing, or situation
  that is mysterious and puzzling
mystery something that remains
  unexplained or secret
problem something difficult to deal
  with or understand
riddle difficult and amusing question
  to which one must guess the answer

perplexity

579 qualm n.

misgiving

compunction pricking of conscience;
  slight regret
pang painful emotion
remorse deep regret for having done
  wrong
scruple doubt or hesitation about
  what is right in a certain situation
self-reproach blaming oneself for a
  fault or offence

580 quarrel n.

bickering quarrelling constantly
  about unimportant things
brawl noisy quarrel, usually
  including fighting
controversy argument about
  something over which there is much
  disagreement
disagreement having different
  opinions and failing to agree
discord lack of agreement, usually
  causing conflict or argument
dissension disagreement leading to a
  quarrel
squabble childish, noisy quarrel
  about unimportant things
wrangle angry, noisy argument

feud *riot* *vendetta*

581 quell v.

subdue   suppress

crush   defeat or subdue completely
pacify   restore to peace and order
put down   suppress by force or
  authority
subjugate   conquer or take power
  over
vanquish   defeat completely

conquer   defeat   stamp out

582 quench v.

damp down   heap ashes on a fire to
  make it burn more slowly
extinguish   put out completely
satisfy   put an end to a demand or
  craving by giving what is required
smother   put out or reduce a fire by
  keeping out air
stifle   prevent from happening or
  continuing

583 question n.

enquiry   request for information
issue   important topic for discussion
leading question   question formed so
  that it suggests the answer
loaded question   question that
  contains a hidden trap
query   question expressing doubt or
  objection

doubt   uncertainty

584 quick adj.

fast   speedy

sudden   happening or done
  unexpectedly or without warning
swift   moving or able to move fast

cursory   fleet of foot

585 quiet adj.

hushed   still and silent
muted   deadened or muffled in sound
subdued   made quieter or less intense

peaceable   soundless

586 quite adv. (i)

*completely   entirely   fully   really
truly*

quite adv. (ii)

rather   somewhat

587 rabble n.

mob

dregs   worst and useless part
hoi polloi   common people; the
  masses
proletariat   class of unskilled wage
  earners
scum   worthless, evil people

*outcasts   ragtag and bobtail
riff-raff*

588 rain n.

deluge   great flood; very heavy fall of
  rain
downpour   heavy, continuous fall of
  rain for a short period
drizzle   very fine, light rain
shower   brief fall of rain or snow
torrent   violently rushing streams of
  water

589 random adj.

aimless   without direction
arbitrary   based on choice or impulse,
  not on reason
casual   happening by chance; made or
  done without forethought

desultory   passing from one thing to
  another without purpose or method
haphazard   careless; slipshod
unmethodical   without order or
  system

chance   *unconsidered*

590   **rank**   adj. (i)

exuberant   growing in great
  abundance and profusion
luxuriant   growing thickly, richly,
  and strongly
overgrown   having grown too much
  or too fast

rank   adj. (ii)

foul-smelling   *foul-tasting*   *offensive*

591   **rash**   adj.

heedless   reckless

foolhardy   boldly but rashly taking
  unnecessary risks
hasty   hurried; speedy
impetuous   acting on impulse too
  hastily and thoughtlessly
incautious   not careful to pay the
  necessary attention
indiscreet   unwisely revealing secrets
  or confidences
injudicious   showing lack of good
  judgement
precipitate   violently hurried

harum-scarum   *hot-headed*
overbold   *uncontrolled*   *unwary*

592   **rather**   adv.

after a fashion   *more exactly*
more truly   *somewhat*   *sooner*
to a certain extent

593   **reach**   v. (i)

arrive at

communicate   connect one thing with
  another; pass on or make known

attain   set foot on

reach   v. (ii)

stretch out

extend   stretch or continue
border on   be next to

594   **read**   v.

peruse   read or examine with care
revise   read again, altering,
  correcting, or improving
scan   look at quickly without careful
  reading
skim   read quickly, noting only the
  chief points
study   spend time in learning or
  considering carefully

dip into   *glance over*   *pore over*
thumb through

595   **ready**   adj.

prepared

available   ready or able to be
  obtained or used
equipped   supplied with what is
  necessary
furnished   provided with what is
  necessary for a special purpose
mature   fully grown or developed
primed   fully prepared for action or
  use
ripe   ready to be picked and eaten or
  used

liable to   *well-provided*

596 real adj.

genuine

actual existing in fact; real
authentic known to be what it is
claimed to be
bona fide genuine, without fraud
realistic based on facts, not on ideas
or illusions
tangible clear and definite, not
imaginary
unfeigned not pretending or false
valid well-grounded in truth

597 really adv.

actually genuinely in fact
in reality positively truly
unquestionably

598 reasonable adj.

equitable fair and just
logical correctly reasoned
plausible seeming to be reasonable or
probable, but not proved
pragmatic treating things from a
practical point of view
rational well-reasoned and sensible
sensible having good sense

commonsensical well-founded

599 rebuke v.

berate scold harshly
chide find fault with in a nagging
way
lecture give a long, solemn scolding
reprehend find fault with; criticize
reprimand give a severe, official
scolding
reprove express disapproval of a
fault or error
upbraid find fault with angrily and
harshly

dress down haul over the coals
read the riot act

600 recover v. (i)

regain

recall take back; call to return from a
place
recapture capture a person or thing
that has escaped or been lost to an
enemy
reclaim demand as the rightful
owner; recover possession of
recoup recover what one has lost or
its equivalent
repossess get back possession
retrieve find and bring back; put
right a mistake, loss, or defeat

recover v. (ii)

recuperate get better from being ill

convalesce pull through

601 red adj.

cardinal deep scarlet
carmine vivid red colour sometimes
with purplish tinge
cerise light clear red
cherry bright red colour of a ripe
cherry
cochineal bright red colouring matter
for food
crimson vivid red
florid having a red or flushed
complexion
magenta deep purplish-red
maroon dark red to purplish-red
ruby colour of a deep red transparent
precious stone
ruddy face with a fresh, healthy
reddish colour
rufous reddish brown
sanguine blood-red; ruddy in
appearance
scarlet vivid red colour, sometimes
with an orange tinge

bloodshot fiery

602   refresh   v.

brace   freshen or fill with energy
reanimate   fill with new strength or courage
rejuvenate   make or become young again
renew   make as good as new; replace
restore   bring back to its original state
resuscitate   restore to consciousness
revive   bring or be brought back to life, consciousness, or strength

energize   revitalize

603   region   n.

department   specialized division of a government or large business
district   part of a country, city, county, or area
locale   place or area in which certain events take place
province   one of the main divisions of some countries for purposes of government control
territory   land under the control of a ruler, state or city
zone   division or area marked off from others

604   regret   v.

bemoan   be very sorry for or over something
bewail   express great sorrow over a person or thing
grieve   feel intense sorrow or distress, especially at someone's death
lament   feel or express remorse or regret
miss   feel the lack or loss of
rue   repent or regret

apologize   repent

605   regular   adj. (i)

accustomed   customary   everyday
habitual   normal   standard   usual

606   regular   adj. (ii)

even   unvarying, level
methodical   orderly and very careful
permanent   meant to last for a long time
regulated   something adjusted so that it works correctly
symmetrical   having balanced proportions
systematic   based on a regular plan or fixed method
uniform   not varying

balanced   orderly   steady

607   reliable   adj.

dependable   trustworthy

608   remarkable   adj.

imposing   grand and impressive
impressive   arousing particular admiration and approval
singular   uncommon; of unusual quality
striking   sure to be noticed

astonishing   astounding

609   remember   v.

commemorate   keep in the memory by means of a celebration or ceremony
memorize   learn so as to remember
recall   bring back to mind
recollect   call something to mind; remember
recognize   know again someone or something one has met before
remind   cause to remember or think of something
reminisce   talk pleasantly about the past

BEAUFORT SCHOOL
SOUTHBOURNE BOURNEMOUTH

610 remiss adj.

negligent

dilatory slow in doing something; causing delay purposely
improvident not providing for future needs
perfunctory done as a duty or routine but without much care
slipshod done as a duty or routine but without much care or interest

careless neglectful slapdash

611 repeat v.

reiterate

paraphrase express something written or said in different words
recapitulate state again the main points of what has been said or discussed
recite say aloud from memory, especially before an audience
regurgitate bring up again
rehearse learn and practise for later performance; say over again
rephrase express in other words, especially more clearly
restate say again, perhaps in different words
retell say again
reword change the wording of

echo parrot reproduce

612 reputation n.

estimation judgement or opinion of a person's worth
face appearance or pretence
name outward appearance or form, not necessarily the truth
repute what is said or thought to be true about someone
standing position in society
status person's position or rank in relation to others

admiration

613 rescue v.

save

deliver set free
free set at liberty; release
liberate set free, especially from control by an authority that is considered to be oppressive
ransom obtain the release of a captive in return for payment

614 resentful adj.

embittered filled with painful and bitter feelings
hostile opposed to; very unfriendly
incensed enraged; made very angry
piqued irritated because of wounded pride
provoked angrily roused to action

antagonistic revengeful

615 resourceful adj.

astute quick at seeing how to gain an advantage
creative producing new and original ideas or things
quick-witted quick to understand and act

616 restless adj.

uneasy unsettled

fidgety nervous and restless
fretful constantly worrying or crying
highly-strung excitable and easily upset
restive restless and resisting control because made impatient by delay or restraint

*edgy itchy jumpy keyed up
on tenterhooks*

617 return v.

come back   go back

backtrack   go back over the same
  path
ebb   flow away from shore; become
  lower or weaker
reappear   come into sight or view
  again
recede   go or shrink back from a
  certain point
reciprocate   give something in return
  for something felt, done, or given
reoccur   happen again
restore   give or put back
retreat   move back, especially when
  forced to
reverse   move in the opposite
  direction
wane   grow smaller in size; decrease
  in vigour, strength, or importance

618 reveal v.

disclose   make known

blab   let out a secret
divulge   make known something
  private or secret
impart   give or make known
  information
inform   give information; tell facts
leak   allow secret or confidential
  information to escape
proclaim   make known publicly or
  officially
publish   make generally known;
  announce formally
release   allow a news story to be
  printed
ventilate   express an opinion publicly
  so that others may consider and
  discuss it

announce   uncover   unmask

619 review v.

reconsider   re-examine

criticize   make judgements about the
  good and bad points
summarize   state briefly the main
  points of
sum up   consider and judge quickly

620 revise v.

correct   go over

amend   correct errors; change for the
  better
edit   prepare written material for
  publication
emend   alter something written to
  remove mistakes
redraft   prepare a second rough
  version of something written
rework   use again in altered form
rewrite   write again in a different way
update   bring up to date

621 rhythm n.

beat   regular repeated sound
cadence   pattern in sound
flow   steady, smooth movement in
  sound
lilt   light, pleasant pattern of rising
  and falling sound
pulse   short, regular single beat
tempo   speed at which music is played

622 rich adj.

moneyed   wealthy

affluent   having plenty of money or
  other possessions
flush   well-supplied with money at
  that moment
lavish   generous or wasteful with
  money
opulent   having or indicating great
  wealth
sumptuous   splendid and costly-
  looking

in clover   well-heeled   well-to-do

623 river n.

beck   brook   cascade   cataract
rapids   reach   rill   rivulet   runnel
sluice   stream   tributary

624 road n.

avenue   wide street or road, often
  lined with trees
boulevard   wide, usually tree-lined,
  road in a city
bypass   road taking traffic round a
  congested area
drive   private road leading to a house
highroad   main road
highway   main route for any form of
  transport
street   public road in a town or village
  with houses on one or both sides
thoroughfare   road for public traffic

motorway

625 rob v.

burgle   break into a building and steal
embezzle   take wrongfully, for one's
  own use, money or property placed
  in one's care
misappropriate   take dishonestly,
  especially for one's own use
peculate   take wrongfully, for one's
  own use, money placed in one's care
pilfer   steal small things or in small
  quantities
plunder   seize goods unlawfully or by
  force
purloin   take something dishonestly
steal   take another person's property
  without right or permission
thieve   steal, especially stealthily and
  without violence

knock off   nick   pinch   shoplift
swipe

626 rope n.

cable   thick, heavy, strong rope, wire,
  or chain
cordage   lines and rigging of a vessel
guy   rope or chain used to keep
  something steady or secured
halyard   rope for raising or lowering a
  rope, flag, or sail
hawser   heavy rope or cable for
  mooring or towing a ship
painter   light rope fastened to the bow
  of a small boat for tying it up
rigging   ropes used to support masts
  and set or work the sails on a ship
tackle   set of ropes and pulleys for
  lifting weights, or working a ship's
  sails

627 rot v.

decay   go or cause to go bad
decompose   break down by bacteria
  or fungi
fester   make or become infected and
  filled with pus
moulder   decay slowly into dust
perish   lose or cause to lose its normal
  qualities
putrefy   rot with a foul smell

628 rotten adj. (i)

abominable   very bad or unpleasant
contemptible   deserving contempt;
  worthless
despicable   deserving to be regarded
  as worthless
detestable   hateful
disgusting   sickening, distasteful, or
  objectionable
loathsome   filling with hatred and
  disgust

rotten adj. (ii)

decayed   decomposed   mouldy

putrid   having rotted or decayed

629 **row** n.

argument   dispute   quarrel   wrangle

630 **rub** v.

buff   polish with something soft
burnish   polish with something hard
  and smooth, especially metal
chafe   make or become sore from
  rubbing
grate   shred into small pieces by
  rubbing against a jagged surface
knead   press and stretch with the
  hands to make soft
massage   press and rub the body to
  lessen pain or stiffness
polish   make, or become, smooth and
  glossy by rubbing
rasp   scrape with a coarse file
scour   clean a surface by hard rubbing
  with a rough material
scrub   rub hard with a stiff brush
smooth   remove roughnesses to make
  an even surface

631 **rude** adj.

discourteous   impolite   unmannerly

brusque   abrupt and rather impolite
curt   rudely short in speech and
  manner
disparaging   speaking of in a slighting
  way; belittling
disrespectful   treating someone as not
  worthy of polite consideration
impertinent   cheeky in speech and
  behaviour
impudent   shamelessly bold
insolent   showing disrespectful
  rudeness
insulting   speaking or acting in a way
  that hurts the feelings or pride of a
  person and rouses their anger
pert   saucy and forward, often in an
  amusing way
uncivil   not polite or obliging

uncouth   ill-mannered; awkward and
  clumsy in manner
vulgar   behaving in a very rude and
  low way

boorish   coarse   indecent   loutish

632 **sad** adj.

unhappy

crestfallen   downcast; very
  disappointed at failure
dejected   in low spirits
depressed   sad and discouraged
despondent   feeling a complete loss of
  hope
miserable   feeling very unhappy,
  uneasy, or uncomfortable
sorrowful   feeling very unhappy over
  loss or wrongdoing

*blue   down-hearted   down-in-the-
dumps   heavy-hearted   woe-begone*

633 **safe** adj.

secure

defended   protected against attack
guarded   kept safe, especially by
  watching for danger
immune   free from; not susceptible to
impregnable   which cannot be entered
  or conquered by attack, especially a
  fortress
invulnerable   that cannot be harmed
protected   kept from harm or injury,
  especially by covering
sheltered   shielded from harm
unassailable   able to withstand
  violent and persistent attack

634 **salty** adj.

briny   full of salt (of water)
brackish   slightly salty (of water)
saline   of, concerned with, consisting
  of, or containing common salt

piquant

635 same adj.

identical

comparable able to be examined or judged against another
corresponding be in agreement with
duplicate exactly like another thing
equivalent equal in amount, force or value
matching like or suitable for use with something else
similar partly or almost the same
synonymous equal or nearly equal in meaning; closely associated with

self-same *unchanging*

636 sarcastic adj.

derisive making fun of in a mocking way
ironic bitterly funny
jeering laughing or shouting at rudely
sardonic humorous in a grim or sarcastic way
taunting making scornful remarks or criticism in order to provoke

637 savage adj.

fierce untamed

barbarous brutal or very cruel; uncivilized
cruel liking to cause pain or suffering
primitive simple or crude
uncivilized behaving in a rough and crude way

diabolical *fiendish*

638 save v. (i)

extricate set free from something that is difficult to escape from
rescue save or bring away from attack, capture, or danger
salvage rescue goods or property from fire or shipwreck

639 save v. (ii)

hoard save and store away
husband save carefully or make the best use of
reserve put aside for a later occasion or for special use
scrape live with no more than the barely necessary money
scrimp save money slowly and with difficulty, especially by living poorly
stockpile keep adding to a stock of goods or materials kept in reserve
withhold keep back on purpose

economize

640 say v.

affirm state as a fact
allege state without being able to prove
announce make known publicly
articulate say or speak distinctly
assert state forcefully
convey make known as an idea or meaning
declare state firmly
express put a thought, feeling, opinion, or fact into words
hint suggest indirectly
mouth say publicly something insincerely; form words with the lips without speaking them aloud
pronounce utter a sound distinctly or in a certain way; declare officially
remark comment on; notice
snap speak with sudden irritation
tell make something known in words

enunciate *utter* *whisper*

641 scarcely adv.

barely hardly not quite only just

642 scare n.

alarm   fright

horror   feeling of great shock and fear
jitters   nervousness before an event
panic   sudden uncontrollable fear
phobia   lasting out-of-the-ordinary
  fear or dread of something
shock   a sudden and violent mental or
  physical impression
terror   very great fear, panic, or dread

643 scent n.

aroma   distinctive, usually pleasant,
  smell
attar   pleasant-smelling oil obtained
  from flowers
bouquet   smell of wine
essence   liquid perfume
fragrance   sweet and pleasant smell
incense   substance that produces a
  sweet smell when burning
odour   characteristic scent or smell
perfume   fragrant liquid for giving a
  pleasant smell, especially to the body
redolence   strong smell
trail   scent or track followed in
  hunting

644 scold v.

admonish   tell off or warn gently
castigate   punish severely in order to
  correct
chastise · punish severely by beating
chide   tell off, but not severely
rebuke   give a short official scolding
reprimand   give a severe official
  scolding
reprove   blame or scold for a fault or
  error
upbraid   find fault with angrily

645 scratch v.

abrade   scrape or wear away by
  rubbing

bark   scrape the skin off accidently
graze   scrape the skin lightly
scrape   hurt or damage a surface by
  rubbing roughly
scuff   make a rough mark or marks on
  a surface

646 scream v.

screech   cry out on a very high, sharp
  note
shriek   cry out with a shrill, piercing
  sound
squall   cry noisily
squawk   make a loud, harsh cry
squeal   utter a long, shrill cry or
  sound
yelp   make a short, sharp, high cry, as
  of pain or excitement

647 sea n.

high seas   open seas not under any
  country's control
main   poetic word for the open ocean
ocean   mass of water that covers most
  of the earth

briny   *Davy Jones's locker*   *the drink*

648 seat n.

bench   long seat for two or more
  people
box   compartment with seats for
  several persons in a theatre
chair   movable seat, with a back, for
  one person
couch   long upholstered seat, usually
  with a back and arms
cushion   bag filled with a soft
  substance on which a person can sit
hassock   thick firm cushion for
  kneeling on in church
pew   long bench with a back for
  sitting on in church

settle long wooden seat with a high
  solid back and a bottom part which is
  a chest
sofa long upholstered seat with a
  back and raised ends or arms
squab stuffed seat or cushion,
  especially as part of a car seat
stall one of the set of seats in the part
  of a theatre nearest to the stage
stool seat without a supporting part
  for one's back or arms

649 see v.

descry notice something far off
discern recognize or perceive clearly
espy catch sight of
notice become aware of
perceive see or notice
sight get a view of, especially after a
  time of looking
spot watch for and take note of

650 seedy adj.

run-down scruffy shabby

degraded reduced in worth;
  disgraced or dishonoured
down-at-heel wearing shoes with
  worn-down heels and old well-worn
  clothes
mangy very untidy and careless in
  appearance
sleazy dirty, cheap and poor-looking
squalid dirty and unpleasant,
  especially because of neglect or
  poverty

651 seek v.

look for search for

ransack search thoroughly or
  roughly
rummage turn things over while
  trying to find something

inquire for nose out

652 seldom adv.

hardly ever infrequently
not often once in a while
rarely scarcely ever

653 selfish adj.

egotistic talking and thinking too
  much about one's own importance
self-centred interested only in oneself
self-indulgent giving way too easily
  to one's own desires for pleasure or
  comfort
self-seeking working only for one's
  own advantage

654 send v.

consign hand over or deliver
  formally; give into someone's care
deliver carry and distribute things to
  several places; hand over, transfer, or
  surrender
forward send on to a new address or
  to a customer
post put a letter etc. into a post office
  or post-box for sending on
remit send money by post
ship send by ship; put or take on
  board a ship for taking somewhere

broadcast radio telegraph televise

655 serious adj.

earnest

acute coming quickly to a dangerous
  condition
critical very serious; of or at a crisis
important having or able to have a
  great effect
meditative thinking seriously or
  deeply
reflective thoughtful

menacing touch-and-go

656 shake v.

chatter make a repeated clicking sound
oscillate move to and fro like a pendulum
quake shake or tremble from fear or unsteadiness
rattle make or cause to make a series of short, sharp, hard sounds
shiver tremble slightly from cold or fear
shudder shake uncontrollably for a moment from fear, cold, or strong dislike
vibrate move unceasingly to and fro, especially rapidly

quiver tremble twitch

657 shameful adj.

belittling implying that something is unimportant or of little value
discreditable unworthy; damaging a good reputation
disgraceful causing loss of respect
dishonourable lacking honesty and principles
humiliating causing a feeling of shame or disgrace
ignoble not noble or honourable in character, aims, or purpose
ignominious shameful to one's pride
improper not seemly or fitting
vile extremely disgusting

658 shine v.

blaze burn with a bright flame
dazzle make unable to see clearly because of too much bright light
flare burn with a sudden irregular flame for a short time
flash give out a sudden bright light
flicker burn or shine unsteadily
glare shine with a strong, unpleasant light
gleam give out a ray of soft light

glimmer give a very faint, unsteady light
glint give out small flashes of light
glisten shine from or as if from a wet surface
glitter shine brightly with flashing points of light
glow send out light and heat without flame
radiate send out light or heat in rays
scintillate give off sparks
shimmer shine with a soft, trembling light
sparkle shine with bright points of light
twinkle shine with an unsteady light that quickly changes from bright to faint and keeps doing this

659 ship n.

boat small ship
ferry boat that carries people and things across a river or other narrow stretch of water
freighter ship or aircraft for carrying goods
liner large passenger ship
merchantman ship carrying goods to be sold wholesale
schooner fast sailing-ship with two or sometimes more masts
steamer large non-naval ship driven by steam power
tanker ship, aircraft, or vehicle for carrying oil or other liquid in bulk
whaler ship engaged in hunting whales

vessel

660 shop n.

boutique small shop selling clothes of the latest fashion
department store large shop divided into separate departments in which different goods are sold

retail store　shop selling goods to customers for their own use, not for resale

supermarket　large self-service shop selling groceries and household goods

wholesale store　large building selling goods in large quantities for resale

workshop　room or building in which manual work or manufacture is carried out

661　shore　n.

beach　shore between high and low water mark with sand or water-worn pebbles; land by a lake or river used for swimming and sunbathing

coast　land next to the sea

foreshore　area along the edge of the sea and where there is grass or buildings

seaboard　part of a country along a sea-coast

seashore　land along the edge of the sea

seaside　sea-coast, especially as a place for holidays

strand　shore or beach

waterside　edge of a river, lake, or sea

662　shortly　adv. (i)

before long　*briefly*　*by and by*　*soon*

shortly　adv. (ii)

concisely　*curtly*　*gruffly*

663　shout　v.

bellow　*call out*　*catcall*　*cry*
cry out　*holler*　*whoop*　*yell*

664　show　v.

bring out　cause to appear; show clearly

demonstrate　show the value or use of

display　arrange a thing so that it can be seen

exhibit　present for the public to see

indicate　point out

present　offer or bring to someone's notice

unveil　uncover; make publicly known

authenticate

665　shy　adj.

bashful　retiring

diffident　hesitating to put oneself or one's ideas forward

reserved　not liking to talk about oneself or show one's feelings

reticent　inclined to be silent; reserved in speech

self-conscious　nervous and uncomfortable about oneself as seen by others

shrinking　unwilling to do something because of shame or dislike

withdrawn　unsociable; unusually reserved

666　silly　adj.

absurd　foolish　ridiculous

asinine　acting like a stupid donkey

farcical　happening as in a humorous play

fatuous　foolish in a self-satisfied way

frivolous　unable to take important matters seriously

idiotic　senseless; very stupid

inane　empty of meaning; senseless

ludicrous　causing laughter and ridicule

nonsensical　not making sense

outrageous shocking; exceeding greatly what is moderate or reasonable
preposterous completely unreasonable or improbable
unwise foolish and thoughtless

childish comical laughable unreasonable

667 sing v.

chant sing or recite a psalm or prayer
croon sing gently in a low, soft voice
hymn sing praises to God or another sacred being
intone say a poem or prayer in a level voice
serenade sing or play in the open air at night, especially to one's lover
trill sing briefly or lightly as a bird
vocalize express with or use the voice
warble sing with trills, runs, and other fancy additions

chirp hum pipe

668 sit v.

bestride have or put a leg on either side of
crouch lower the body close to the ground by bending knees and back
hunker down sit on one's heels
lounge stand or sit in a leaning, lazy manner
perch rest or place on something narrow or high
squat crouch with knees drawn up closely
straddle sit or stand across a thing with the legs wide apart

669 size n.

bulk mass, volume
dimensions length, breadth and height

magnitude greatness of size or importance
proportions measurements and shape as they relate to one another
volume amount of space that a three-dimensional thing occupies or contains; strength or power of sound

measurements

670 sketchy adj.

brief in as few words as possible
preliminary coming before a main action or event
preparatory done in order to get ready for something
provisional arranged or agreed upon for the time being, but possibly to be altered later
superficial lacking in thoroughness and care

crude incomplete

671 skill n.

adeptness high degree of skill
competence ability to do satisfactorily what is needed
dexterity skill in handling things
efficiency satisfactory results produced with little waste or effort
expertise special skill, knowledge, or judgement
handiness cleverness with one's hands
know-how practical skill or knowledge in a particular activity

adroitness facility faculty knack

672 sleep v.

catnap take a very short, light sleep
doze sleep lightly
drowse be half asleep
nap have a short sleep during the day
slumber sleep peacefully

snooze   take a short, light sleep during the day

nod off   take a siesta

673   **slogan**   n.

catchphrase   a few words which become popular for a time and used by everybody
motto   short sentence expressing the aims and ideals of a family, country, or institution; verse or riddle inside a paper cracker

674   **slow**   adj. (i)

dawdling   walking slowly and idly; wasting time
deliberate   unhurried and careful
lagging   failing to keep up with others
leisurely   relaxed without hurry
plodding   working at a slow but steady rate
unhurried   done with ample time and without haste

675   **slow**   adj. (ii)

backward   having made less than normal progress
dense   stupid
doltish   slow-thinking and foolish
dull   slow in understanding
obtuse   mentally slow or emotionally insensitive
simple   feeble-minded
unintelligent   without much ability to reason or understand

dull-witted   slow-witted   stupid thick

676   **sly**   adj.

artful   crafty   cunning   wily

cagey   cautious about giving information; secretive

shady   of very doubtful honesty or character
slippery   not to be trusted or relied upon

sneaky

677   **small**   adj.

little

diminutive   remarkably small
dwarfed   much below the average height or size
miniature   greatly reduced in size; made or represented on a small scale
minute   extremely small
pint-sized   very small
short   measuring little from end to end in space or time; of small stature
tiny   very small

678   **smelly**   adj.

fetid   having a stale, sickening, decaying smell
malodorous   having a bad smell
nauseating   having a sickening or disgusting smell
noisome   offensively smelly
putrid   very decayed and bad smelling
rank   highly offensive and disagreeable

foul-smelling   stinking

679   **smile**   v.

beam   smile brightly and happily
grimace   twist the face in pain or disgust, or to cause amusement
grin   smile broadly showing the teeth
simper   smile in a silly, unnatural way
smirk   smile in a false or too self-satisfied way

680 smooth adj

burnished shiny and smooth;
  polished by rubbing
glossy smooth and reflecting the light
sleek smooth and well-cared for in
  appearance

*glassy icy oily polished satiny
silky*

681 so adv. (i)
very

so conj. (ii)
therefore thus

682 soft adj.

flabby too soft and limp
flaccid hanging loose or wrinkled
pliable bending easily without
  breaking
pliant supple

*crumbly doughy jelly-like limp
over-ripe pulpy spongy squashy
squishy*

683 solid adj.

congealed semi-solid instead of liquid
crystallized clear, definite, and solid
  in form
firm hard, solid structure
impenetrable unable to be gone into
  or through
impermeable which substances,
  especially liquids, cannot get
  through
insoluble unable to be dissolved
stable not easily moved or changed

hard

684 sometime adj.
erstwhile former late

685 sometimes adv.

at times now and again
occasionally on occasion

686 somewhat adv.

fairly in part rather
to some extent

687 song n.

air simple tune for singing or playing
anthem religious song sung in church
  by a choir
ballad song or poem that tells a story,
  usually with a chorus
chant psalm or prayer sung or recited
descant tune sung or played, usually
  higher, in accompaniment to the main
  tune
ditty short, simple song
folk-song song handed down by
  word of mouth; modern imitation of
  this
lyric words of a song; short poem
melody song or tune; clearly
  recognizable tune in a larger
  arrangement of notes
round part-song in which the voices
  follow each other at equal intervals
  at the same pitch
shanty song formerly sung by sailors
  in time to their work
spiritual religious folk-song, sung
  originally by American negroes
tune number of musical notes, one
  after the other, that produce a
  pleasing pattern of sounds

688 soon adv.
presently shortly

ere long forthwith

689 sore adj.

aching having a continuous, dull pain
burning having a very hot feeling
inflamed red and swollen because hurt or diseased
painful suffering great discomfort
raw having the surface of the skin rubbed off
sensitive easily hurt
smarting stinging pain that lasts for some time
stinging feeling a sudden, sharp pain
tender painful when touched; sensitive

690 sound n.

blare harsh, loud sound
blast sudden loud sound as of a trumpet or car horn
chime sound made by a set of bells
clank short, loud sound of metal striking metal
clatter number of rapid short knocks
clink thin, sharp sound like glasses striking together
creak harsh squeak like that of an unoiled hinge
grate harsh noise made by rubbing
groan long, deep sound caused by the movement of wood or metal parts heavily loaded
howl long, loud wailing cry of a dog; similar noise made by a strong wind or an electrical amplifier
knell sound of a bell tolled solemnly after a death or at a funeral
moan low, mournful sound
peal loud ringing of bells or burst of thunder
rasp harsh, grating sound
ring loud, clear sound like a bell
roar deep, loud, continuing sound like that made by a lion
rumble deep, heavy, rolling sound
tinkle short, light, metallic sounds

toll sound of a bell ringing slowly and repeatedly

691 sour adj.

curdled milk separated into soft, thick lumps and clear liquid
rancid tasting or smelling like stale fat

acid   tart   vinegary

692 space n.

area   expanse

capaciousness ability to hold a lot
capacity amount that something can hold
immensity enormous expanse
interval space between two objects or moments in time
leeway room for free movement within limits
spaciousness great amount of room
vastness very great in area or size

acreage   elbow-room

693 special adj.

distinctive not commonly found elsewhere
memorable worth remembering; noticeable
outstanding exceptionally good; better than others
pre-eminent above all others
rare very uncommon; seldom found or occurring
select picked out as best or most suitable

extraordinary   noteworthy out-of-the-ordinary

694 spectator n.

beholder   bystander   eye-witness observer   onlooker

695 speechless adj.

dumbfounded unable to speak because of surprise or lack of understanding
dumbstruck temporarily deprived of speech through shock or surprise
inarticulate unable to express oneself clearly
non-plussed not knowing what to think or do

tongue-tied

696 speed n.

rapidity swiftness

alacrity prompt and eager readiness
dispatch speed and effectiveness of action
velocity rate of movement, especially in a given direction

697 spend v.

pay out

disburse pay out money
expend use up or spend
lay out spend money for a special purpose
splurge spend money freely and with great show
squander spend foolishly and wastefully

dish out *fork out* *shell out*

698 spite n.

animosity powerful and active dislike or hostility
antagonism active opposition or hatred between people or groups
ill will unkind feeling
malevolence evil feeling towards others
malice wish or intention to harm others

pique feeling of hurt pride
venom strong, bitter feeling; hatred

envy *jealousy* *resentment*

699 spoil v. (i)

damage harm impair

deface spoil by writing or making marks on
disfigure spoil the appearance
mar damage or spoil
tarnish make or become dull or discoloured
vandalize damage property wilfully or maliciously

ruin

700 spoil v. (ii)

coddle give way too much to the desires of someone
dote on show too much fondness for
indulge allow people to have what they wish
pamper treat too kindly
pervert lead astray from right behaviour or beliefs

overprotect

701 stale adj.

musty smelling unpleasantly old
wilted limp and drooping
withered shrivelled; without freshness or vitality

mouldy *tasteless*

702 stare v.

eye look at carefully, warily, or with desire
gape stare with open mouth in surprise or wonder
glare stare angrily or fiercely

goggle   stare stupidly or fixedly, as in astonishment
watch   keep one's eyes fixed on

703   stay   v.

remain

abide   remain; dwell
endure   remain in existence; last
lodge   stay, usually for a short time, and paying rent
sojourn   live for a time in a place
survive   live after the death of another

704   stealthy   adj.

clandestine   done secretly, often for an unlawful reason
covert   concealed or secret
furtive   sly and secretive
surreptitious   done or gained in secret, or by dishonest means
undercover   done or acting in secret

705   steep   adj.

abrupt   very steep or sudden
precipitous   dangerously steep like the edge of a cliff
sheer   straight up or down with no slope

706   steep   v.

soak

brew   make beer; make tea ready for drinking
immerse   put completely into water
marinate   steep meat or fish in seasoned flavoured liquid before cooking
pickle   preserve in vinegar or brine
saturate   make thoroughly wet
seethe   bubble or surge as in boiling
souse   plunge or soak in liquid

707   stern   adj.

severe   strict

austere   severely simple and plain
harsh   showing cruelty or lack of kindness
relentless   always without pity or let-up
rigorous   harsh and lacking in mercy
unsparing   unmerciful
unyielding   not giving way to pressure or influence

flinty   hard-hearted   unbending

708   stirring   adj.

exciting   rousing   stimulating

dramatic   very exciting and impressive
gripping   keeping a tight hold on a person's attention
thrilling   causing a wave of fear, excitement, or pleasure

intoxicating   melodramatic

709   stomach   n.

belly   tummy

abdomen   part of body containing stomach, bowels and digestive organs
bowels   inner, lower part of the abdomen
entrails   inside parts of an animal, especially the bowels
guts   internal organs of the abdomen
innards   stomach and bowels
intestine   tube carrying food away from the stomach
paunch   protruding belly
pot-belly   large rounded stomach

beer-belly   bread basket

710 stop v. (i)

cease   end   finish

abandon   give up; cease work on
desist from   not to do any more of
discontinue   put an end to; come to an
  end
quit   go away from; leave; abandon
  or give up a task

711 stop v. (ii)

bar   block movement or action; not to
  allow
check   stop or slow the motion of
  suddenly
curb   control or limit
foil   prevent from succeeding
hamper   prevent free movement or
  activity
prevent   hinder; stop
prohibit   forbid by law or rule
restrain   control by holding back
suppress   put an end to the activity of;
  keep from being known or seen
thwart   oppose successfully

barricade   blockade

712 storm n.

tempest

blizzard   long severe snowstorm
cloudburst   sudden violent rainstorm
hurricane   storm with violent wind
monsoon   seasonal heavy rains and
  winds in South East Asia
tornado   violent and destructive
  whirlwind advancing in a narrow
  path
typhoon   violent tropical storm in the
  western Pacific

duststorm   sandstorm   thunderstorm

713 story n.

account   tale

allegory   story or description in which
  the characters represent good and bad
  qualities
anecdote   short, amusing, or
  interesting story about a real person
  or event
autobiography   book written by
  oneself about one's own life
biography   book of a person's life
  written by someone else
chronicle   record of historical events
  in the order they happened
epic   long poem, or other work of
  literature, telling of heroic deeds
  or history
fable   short story not based on fact,
  often with animals as characters and
  teaching a moral
fiction   invented story
history   record or account of past
  events in the order in which they
  happened
legend   story handed down from the
  past which may or may not be true
memoirs   written account of events
  that one has lived through
myth   traditional story containing
  ideas or beliefs about ancient times
  or about natural events
narration   the telling of facts, events,
  or a story
novel   book-length story about
  invented people
parable   story told to illustrate a
  moral or spiritual truth
saga   long story with many episodes

novelette   science fiction

714 strange adj.

unusual

alien   foreign; very unfamiliar and
  strange
curious   strange and unusual

odd   unusual and peculiar in appearance or character
outlandish   looking or sounding strange or foreign
peculiar   strange and distinct from others
quaint   odd in a pleasing way; attractive through being unusual or old-fashioned
unfamiliar   not well known; not often seen or experienced

uncommon

715   **strong**   adj.

powerful

brawny   strong and muscular
burly   strong and heavily built
hardy   able to bear cold, hard work, or difficult conditions
herculean   possessing very great strength
mighty   having great power or strength; very great in size
robust   healthy, strong, and vigorous
strapping   big, tall, and healthy-looking

beefy   hefty   muscle-bound

716   **subject**   n.

angle   point of view
gist   essential points or general sense, especially of a long statement
matter   contents of something written or spoken as distinct from its form
proposition   suggestion; something to be dealt with
text   original words of a speech, article, or book
theme   main idea or topic in a talk or piece of writing
thesis   statement or theory put forward and supported by argument
topic   subject for a speech, conversation, or written work

717   **successful**   adj.

booming   growing rapidly in value, importance, and prosperity
flourishing   growing and developing healthily
lucrative   bringing in plenty of money
productive   tending or able to make things, especially in large quantities
profitable   bringing money or benefits
prosperous   financially successful
thriving   doing very well

718   **suddenly**   adv.

abruptly   suddenly and surprisingly
hastily   said, made, or done too quickly
instantly   at once
unexpectedly   surprisingly and unforeseen

719   **suggest**   v.

advocate   be or speak in favour of
hint   refer indirectly to
imply   suggest without stating directly
introduce   make known or mention for the first time
propose   put forward for consideration
recommend   praise as being good for a purpose
submit   offer for consideration or decision

bring up   moot   put forward

720   **sulky**   adj.

morose   gloomy and unsociable
peevish   easily annoyed
petulant   showing childish temper for no reason
resentful   feeling bitter or insulted
sullen   silently showing dislike or ill temper

721 supply v

provide

cater provide food and drink for payment at a public or private party
distribute divide among several; spread or scatter
equip supply with what is necessary
furnish supply with what is necessary for a special purpose
provision provide with food and supplies
replenish fill up again
satisfy give a person what he demands or needs; fulfil or comply with

722 suspect v.

distrust lack belief in; be suspicious of
doubt be uncertain about
infer get the meaning from something by reasoning
presume take as a fact without proof

mistrust smell a rat

723 swear v. (i)

depose give evidence, especially on oath in court
pledge promise solemnly
promise declare that one will do or not do a thing
testify bear witness to a fact; give evidence under oath
vow promise solemnly

swear v. (ii)

curse exlaim in anger with oaths and indecent words

724 swollen adj.

distended enlarged

bloated unpleasantly swollen with fat, gas, or liquid
dilated made or become wider or larger
dropsical swollen by watery fluid in the tissues of the body
expanded made or become larger
inflated filled and swollen with air or gas
puffy slightly swollen
turgid swollen by liquid or inner pressure

over-stuffed

725 talk v.

address direct a remark or written statement to
blurt out say suddenly and without thinking
chat talk in a friendly manner
chatter talk quickly and at length about unimportant matters
confer discuss and compare opinions
consult seek information or advice
converse exchange thoughts and opinions; talk
declaim speak or say impressively or dramatically
digress depart from the main subject temporarily in speaking or writing
discuss consider by talking or writing about
enthuse show a strong interest and admiration through talking
gush express admiration or pleasure in a great flow of words foolishly and without true feeling
harangue address in an angry or forceful way, especially to blame the listeners
jabber talk quickly and not clearly
lecture give a talk to a group
maunder talk in a rambling, aimless way

pontificate   speak or write as if one's
  judgement is the only correct one
prattle   chatter in a childish way
rage   talk or shout in a very angry
  way
rant   make a speech loudly, violently
  and showily
rave   talk wildly as if mad
spout   pour out in a stream of words
tattle   gossip about another's personal
  matters or secrets

flare up   fulminate   gossip   mumble
mutter   preach   ramble   stammer
relate

726 tame adj. (i)

broken-in   made tame or disciplined
  by training
controllable   able to be managed
docile   obedient and easily taught or
  led
domesticated   animals trained to live
  with and be kept by man
trained   taught and accustomed to do
  something

tame adj. (ii)

unexciting

727 taste v.

relish   savour or enjoy to the full
savour   taste slowly and purposefully
  with enjoyment
try   test on one's palate to see if one
  likes it

728 teach v.

coach   improve the skills or
  knowledge
cram   study for an examination by
  hastily memorizing
educate   train and develop the mind,
  abilities, and character

indoctrinate   fill a person's mind with
  particular ideas
instruct   give a person instruction in a
  subject or skill
school   discipline or control
train   give teaching or practice,
  especially in an art, profession, or
  skill
tutor   give private instruction to a
  single pupil or very small group

729 teacher n.

coach   person who trains sportsmen
  and athletes, or a student for an
  examination
educationalist   an expert in
  educational methods
governess   female teacher who lives
  with a family and educates their
  children at home
guru   influential or revered teacher
instructor   one who gives information
  or knowledge, or teaches particular
  skills
lecturer   person who teaches in a
  college or university
mentor   trusted adviser
pedagogue   one who teaches in a dull,
  detailed and unimaginative way
schoolmaster   male teacher in a
  school
schoolmistress   female teacher in a
  school
trainer   person who trains athletes or
  animals
tutor   private teacher; university
  teacher directing the studies of
  undergraduates

730 tease v.

annoy   make a little angry, especially
  by repeated acts
bedevil   trouble greatly
harass   trouble and annoy continually
pester   annoy with frequent requests
  or questions

torment   cause persistent distress to mind or body
vex   irritate and worry

make fun of

731   telescope   n.

binoculars   instrument with lenses for both eyes, making distant objects seem nearer
field-glasses   large binoculars for outdoor use
microscope   instrument with lens that magnifies objects or details too small to be seen by the naked eye
opera-glasses   small binoculars for use at the theatre
periscope   long tube containing mirrors so that a person lower down, especially in a submarine, can see what is above him
spy-glass   small telescope

732   tell   v.

delineate   portray in words, especially with detail and exactness
depict   picture in words
describe   give an account of what something is like
explain   make plain or clear; show the meaning of
narrate   tell a story; give an account of
portray   describe in words or represent in a play
recount   tell in detail
relate   tell a story
report   give a factual account
sketch   describe roughly with few details

733   telling   adj.

effective   revealing

cogent   compelling belief or agreement

convincing   making a person feel certain that something is true
forceful   strongly persuasive
suggestive   bringing new ideas to the mind, in addition to what is expressed
weighty   showing or deserving earnest thought

734   temper   n.

anger   feeling of great annoyance or hostility
indignation   anger aroused by something thought to be unjust or wicked
irritability   state of being easily and quickly annoyed by small things
peevishness   sulky fretfulness
petulance   state of unreasonable impatience
surliness   state of bad temper and bad manners
tantrum   outburst of bad temper, especially in a child
wrath   great anger

hot-headedness

735   tempt   v.

captivate   capture the fancy of
entice   attract or persuade by offering something pleasant
infatuate   inspire or fill with foolish, shallow, or extravagant passion
lure   attract or tempt away from what one should do
seduce   persuade, especially into wrongdoing, by making it seem attractive

736   terrific   adj.

excellent   exceptional   first-class marvellous   outstanding   sensational smashing   splendid   spot-on wonderful

737 then adv.

*after that   at that time   from then on
in that case   next   subsequently
thereupon*

738 therefore adv.

*accordingly   because of
consequently   for that reason   hence
on account of   so   thus*

739 thief n.

blackmailer   person who makes
another give money by threatening to
reveal a guilty secret
burglar   person who breaks into a
building to steal
cat-burglar   thief who enters buildings
by climbing walls or drainpipes
con man   person who makes people
believe in him to cheat them
cracksman   expert in breaking into
safes
housebreaker   thief who enters houses
by force, especially during the day
mugger   person who robs another by
violence, especially in a public place
pilferer   thief who steals small things
sneak-thief   person who takes things
within reach without using force
swindler   person who cheats in a
business deal

*pick-pocket   poacher   rustler
shoplifter   smuggler*

740 thin adj.

emaciated   having become very thin
from illness or starvation
gangling   tall, thin, and awkward-
looking
gaunt   bony and emaciated in
appearance
haggard   looking exhausted and
careworn from prolonged worry,
illness, or lack of sleep
lanky   ungracefully lean and tall
lean   without much flesh
scraggy   thin and bony
scrawny   without much flesh on the
bones
skinny   very thin
slender   delicately or gracefully thin
in the body
slim   attractively and lightly built
spare   thin and lean
spindly   long, thin, and weak-looking
weedy   weakly in appearance
wiry   lean but tough and strong
wizened   dried up and wrinkled with
age

half-starved   underfed   wasted

741 thing n.

*apparatus   article   contrivance
device   gadget   instrument
machine   mechanism   object   stuff
substance   tool*

742 think v.

analyse   examine carefully in order to
find out about
brood   think long and deeply,
resentfully, or sadly
conceive   form an idea or plan in the
mind
consider   think about carefully in
order to make a decision
deliberate   think over or discuss
carefully before reaching a decision
imagine   think, believe, or guess
meditate   think deeply, seriously, and
quietly
muse   reflect about, or ponder on,
usually in silence
picture   form a mental image of
ponder   think something over
thoroughly

reason use one's ability to think and draw conclusions
reflect remind oneself of past events, consider

believe *concentrate on* *mull over*

743 through prep. & adv.

between from end to end
from side to side *throughout*

744 throw v.

cast throw off or away
chuck throw carelessly or casually
fling throw violently, angrily or hurriedly
heave lift or haul with great effort
hurl throw with force
pitch hurl, throw, cast, or fling
shy throw with a quick movement
sling throw, especially roughly or with effort
toss throw lightly, carelessly, or easily

catapult *pitchfork*

745 tie v.

bind tie or fasten together securely
lash secure firmly with cord
moor fasten a boat to a fixed object with ropes or an anchor
picket secure or enclose with a stake or stakes
stake fasten or strengthen with sticks or posts
strap secure with a strip of leather or other flexible material
tether fasten an animal with a rope or chain to limit movement
truss tie so as to prevent all movement
yoke harness two animals together by means of a wooden crosspiece; couple, unite

bandage *make fast*

746 tight adj.

compressed forced into less space; squeezed tightly together
cramped put or kept in too narrow a space, without room to move
jammed packed tightly into a small space
taut stretched firmly, not slack

skin-tight

747 time n.

age length of time a person has lived or a thing has existed
date time shown by the number of the day, month, and year
epoch particular period of history
era period of time named after or starting from an important event
instant an exact point of time; the present moment
juncture point in time, especially a critical one
occasion time at which a particular event takes place
season time of year when something is common or plentiful, or when a particular activity takes place

moment *period*

748 tired adj.

bored fed-up and not interested
exhausted tired out and lacking all energy
fatigued greatly tired because of much hard work or exercise
weary very tired, especially from long effort

all in *dead tired* *dog-tired* *done in*
fagged out *ready to drop* *spent*
worn-out

749 too adv. (i)

also   as well   in addition   moreover

too adv. (ii)
excessively

750 top n.

apex   crown   summit

acme   highest point of development,
   success, or perfection
brow   ridge at the top of a slope or hill
crest   top of a slope, hill, mountain,
   or wave
pinnacle   highest point
zenith   highest point of hope,
   achievement or fortune

751 touch v.

brush   touch lightly in passing
caress   give a loving touch or kiss
feel   explore by touch
finger   feel or handle with one's
   fingers
handle   touch, feel, or move with the
   hands
press   apply weight or force steadily
   to a thing
stroke   pass the hand over gently,
   especially to give pleasure

fondle   paw   pet

752 tough adj.

durable   not wearing out or decaying
   quickly
leathery   like hard skin
stubborn   strong-willed and not easy
   to control or deal with
sturdy   strongly-built

hard-boiled   obstinate

753 tower n.

belfry   space in a tower where bells
   are hung
citadel   fortress overlooking a city
cupola   small dome on a roof
fortress   building, place, or town
   strengthened for defence
minaret   tall, slender tower forming
   part of a mosque
obelisk   tall, pointed stone pillar set
   up as a monument
pagoda   Indian or Far Eastern temple,
   usually shaped like a pyramid and
   having many storeys
pyramid   ancient stone building with
   a flat, usually square, base and
   sloping sides that meet at the top
spire   tall roof rising steeply to a point
   on top of a tower
steeple   church tower rising to a high,
   sharp point
turret   small tower on a building or
   defensive wall

754 trick v.

cheat

bamboozle   mystify with a trick
bemuse   puzzle completely
deceive   make someone believe
   something which is false
defraud   deceive so as to get
   something illegally
dupe   deceive, especially by trickery
mislead   lead astray; deceive
outmanoeuvre   put in a position of
   disadvantage
outwit   get the better of a person by
   one's cleverness or craftiness

hoodwink   misinform

755 truly adv.

actually   certainly   genuinely
indeed   loyally   really   sincerely
surely   truthfully   undoubtedly

756 try v.

attempt

endeavour try hard and steadily
essay make an effort to accomplish
something
strive struggle hard to get or conquer
undertake agree or promise to do
something; make oneself responsible
for
venture risk going somewhere or
doing something dangerous

757 turn v.

circle travel round, returning to the
starting point
gyrate swing round and round a fixed
point
pivot turn on a central point or shaft
revolve move or cause to move
around a centre or axis
rotate turn or cause to turn round a
fixed point
spin turn or cause to turn rapidly on
its axis
swivel turn or swing as if on a central
shaft
wheel move in circles or curves

758 ugly adj.

deformed badly or not normally
shaped
disfigured with the appearance
spoiled
grisly causing fear, horror, or disgust
gruesome shocking and sickening
ill-favoured unattractive
monstrous of unnaturally large size
or strange shape and appearance
mutilated maimed or damaged,
especially with an essential part cut
off
nauseating sickening and disgusting
unsightly not pleasant to look at

repulsive

759 unconcerned adj.

aloof not joining in; distant in feeling
or interest
distant remote in manner; unfriendly
impassive not feeling or showing
emotion
indifferent not caring about or
noticing
uninterested without interest
uninvolved not taking part or
interested in the affairs of others

preoccupied *unsympathetic*
unworried

760 under prep.

below   beneath   underneath

761 understand v.

comprehend

apprehend grasp the meaning
discern see or understand, especially
with difficulty
fathom get at the true meaning
grasp succeed in understanding

get the picture

762 unfair adj.

unjust

biased influenced unfairly for or
against
one-sided seeing only one side of a
question
prejudiced having an unreasoning
opinion or dislike
undeserved not meriting a reward or
punishment
unjustifiable not having a good reason
for

unsporting

763 unsure adj.

uncertain

dubious doubtful
sceptical inclined to disbelieve things
unconvinced uncertain that
  something is true
undecided not yet having made up
  one's mind

doubtful suspicious unconfident

764 up-to-date adj.

*current fashionable fresh
in the swim latest modern
present-day recent*

765 urgent adj.

critical of or at a crisis
crucial of decisive importance
demanding needing a lot of attention,
  patience and skill
essential absolutely necessary
imperative extremely urgent or
  important
vital essential to the existence,
  success, or working of something

high-priority pressing serious

766 use v.

employ use the services of; make use
  of
exploit work or develop; use for
  one's own advantage and other
  people's disadvantage
manipulate handle, manage, or use a
  thing skilfully
manoeuvre guide a thing skilfully or
  craftily
operate control the function; cause to
  work
ply wield or use a tool or weapon;
  work at a job or trade
utilize make use of or find a use for

wield hold and use with the hands;
  have and use power

consume expend

767 useful adj.

effective producing the desired result
functional made for practical use
  without ornamentation
practical convenient in actual use
serviceable suitable for ordinary use
  or wear

advantageous convenient usable

768 useless adj.

fruitless producing little or no result
impracticable cannot be used in
  practice
ineffective not producing the desired
  result
ineffectual having no or very little
  effect
unavailing not being of any help or
  advantage

futile unprofitable unserviceable

769 usual adj.

customary

established widely or permanently
  accepted
habitual done regularly
routine regular and not exciting
set fixed or decided

accustomed normal

770 value n.

worth

usefulness

771 vehicle n.

automobile bicycle bus car carriage cart conveyance jeep lorry moped motorcycle sledge tank tractor train tram trolley truck wagon

772 very adv.

deeply exceedingly exceptionally extremely notably

773 view n.

feature any typical or noticeable part of the scenery
outlook view on which one looks out
panorama view over a wide area
prospect extensive view of a landscape
scene landscape or view as seen by a spectator
setting surroundings in which something is placed
spectacle striking or impressive sight
vision rare or beautiful sight
vista view, especially one seen through a long, narrow opening, such as an avenue of trees

landscape seascape scenery skyscape

774 vow n.

oath solemn promise; solemn undertaking to do something
pledge formal promise or agreement
testimony formal statement that something is true; information given on oath

avowal promise undertaking word-of-honour

775 vulgar adj.

indecent offending against recognized standards; unseemly
lewd treating sexual matters in a low way
obscene indecent in a repulsive or very offensive way

filthy immodest improper shameless smutty

776 wait v.

await wait for; be in store or ready for
loiter move about idly with frequent stops
postpone keep from happening until a later time
procrastinate put off action until a later time
tarry delay in coming or going

dally dawdle kill time

777 wakeful adj.

attentive taking careful notice
observant quick at noticing things

on guard watchful wide-awake

778 walk v.

amble walk at an easy, gentle rate
mince walk with dainty steps in an affected manner
pace walk with slow, regular steps
pad walk softly with the feet flat on the ground
plod walk with heavy, usually slow, steps
prowl move stealthily around as if in search of prey or plunder
saunter walk in an unhurried way
shamble walk or move along in an awkward or unsteady way

shuffle walk without lifting the feet clear of the ground

sidle move in a furtive or stealthy manner; edge along

slink move quietly and secretly, as if fearful or ashamed

stagger move or go unsteadily, as if about to fall

stride walk with long steps

stroll walk slowly for pleasure

strut walk in a pompous, self-satisfied way

swagger walk with a swinging movement, as if proud

tread step in, on, over or across

trudge walk with heavy steps, slowly and with effort

waddle walk with short steps, rocking slightly from side to side

hike   *limp*   *march*   *ramble*   *toddle*
totter   *tramp*

779 **wall** n.

barricade wall hastily built as a defence

bulkhead upright partition in a ship or aircraft

bulwark strong wall of earth built as a defence

dry-wall wall built of stones without the aid of mortar

dyke long wall or embankment to keep back water and prevent flooding

embankment long mound of earth or a stone structure to keep a river from spreading, or to carry a road or railway

paling fencing made of wooden posts or railings

rampart wide bank protecting a fort or city

screen upright structure used to conceal, protect or divide something

stockade protective fence of strong upright stakes

partition

780 **want** v.

covet desire eagerly, especially something belonging to another person

crave have a very strong longing for

desire wish or want very much

lack be without or not have a thing when it is needed

long for have an intense, persistent wish for

need want for some useful purpose

pine for become ill, feeble, or thin through longing

require need; depend on for success or fulfilment

fancy   *wish for*   *yearn for*

781 **war** n.

battle fight between enemies or opposing groups

campaign series of military operations with a set purpose, usually in one area

civil war war between groups of citizens of the same country

crusade struggle or movement against something believed to be bad

guerrilla warfare fighting or harassment by small groups acting independently against regular troops or police

hostilities acts of warfare

total war war involving civilians as well as the armed forces

warfare state of war; being engaged in war

Armageddon

782 **warm** adj.

close lacking fresh or freely-moving air

lukewarm slightly warmer than cold

mild gently agreeable weather

muggy unpleasantly damp and warm

snug warm and cosy

tepid only slightly warm

783 wash v.

clean

bath   cleanse   launder   mop
rinse   scrub   shampoo   shower
soak   sponge   swab

784 waste v.

dissipate use up foolishly
fritter away waste little by little,
  especially on trivial things
splurge spend money freely and
  showily
squander spend wastefully or
  extravagantly

deplete   exhaust   misspend

785 watch v.

gaze look long and steadily
observe see and notice; watch
  carefully
ogle look at with great, especially
  sexual, interest
spy keep watch secretly
stare look fixedly with the eyes wide
  open
view watch or inspect carefully
witness be present and notice

786 wave n.

bore very large wave caused by a tide
  running up a narrow river
breaker heavy ocean wave that
  breaks on the coast
chop short, broken waves
comber long, curling wave
ground swell heavy, slow-moving
  waves caused by a distant or recent
  storm
surf white foam of waves breaking
  on a rock or shore
swell heaving of the sea with waves
  that do not break

tidal wave unusually large incoming
  wave, often caused by high winds,
  spring tides, or an earthquake

787 weak adj.

decrepit weak or in bad condition
  from old age or hard work
delicate liable to illness; easily
  injured; requiring careful handling
diluted made less concentrated by
  adding water or a thinner
feeble without strength or force
flimsy easily broken or destroyed
fragile easily damaged; not strong
frail physically weak
infirm weak in body or mind,
  especially from age or illness
puny undersized, feeble

788 wear v.

erode wear away gradually
fray make clothes or material worn
  so that there are loose threads,
  especially at the edge
rub wear by moving to and fro

789 weighty adj. (i)

heavy

bulky very large and unwieldly;
  taking up much space
cumbersome clumsy to wear, carry,
  or manage
hefty large, heavy, and difficult to
  move
massive very large and heavy, and
  usually solid
ponderous huge and unwieldly
unwieldy awkward to move or
  control because of its size, shape,
  or weight

790 weighty adj. (ii)

important

cogent convincing, compelling belief
momentous of very great importance
  or seriousness
persuasive having the power to
  influence others
significant of noticeable importance
  or effect
telling very effective

influential

791 wet adj.

drenched completely wet through
saturated unable to hold any more
  liquid
soaked made thoroughly wet
sodden heavy with wetness
soggy unpleasantly full of moisture
sopping completely soaked and
  dripping
waterlogged so full of water it will
  barely float; earth so wet it cannot
  be worked

792 white adj.

*chalky   creamy   ivory   marble
milky   pearly   snow-white   snowy*

793 wide adj.

all-embracing including everything
broad large across
expansive widely spread
extensive large in area
spacious having a lot of room
wide-ranging covering an extensive
  area
world-wide extending through the
  whole world

widespread

794 wind n.

cyclone very violent wind moving
  quickly in a circle round a calm centre
doldrums ocean regions near the
  equator where there is little or no
  wind
draught current or flow of air
gale very strong wind
gust sudden rush of wind
squall sudden storm of wind,
  especially with rain, snow, or sleet
trade wind belt of winds blowing
  towards the equator
zephyr soft, gentle wind

795 wise adj.

enlightened having true
  understanding
erudite having or showing great
  learning
judicious showing good sense
perceptive quick to notice and
  understand
sagacious having deep understanding
  and judgement
scholarly concerned with serious,
  detailed study; having great
  knowledge of a subject

796 wonderful adj.

*amazing   astounding   awe-inspiring
extraordinary   fantastic   magnificent
marvellous   miraculous   remarkable*

797 wood n.

afforestation process of planting with
  trees to form a forest
coppice wood of small trees and
  undergrowth, grown for periodic
  cutting
copse another word for coppice
forest large wooded area having a
  thick growth of trees and plants
grove small group of trees

plantation   area of land on which cultivated trees or plants are grown

scrub   low-growing plants including bushes and short trees growing in poor soil

spinney   small wood

thicket   number of shrubs and small trees growing close together

timber   trees for building or paper-making

woodland   wooded country

798   work   n. (i)

labour

drudgery   hard, dull work

grind   hard, monotonous work

handiwork   work needing the skilful use of the hands

legwork   working that involves travelling on foot

odd-job   work that is not regular or fixed

spadework   hard work done in preparation for something

task   piece of work to be done

undertaking   task or enterprise; agreement to do something

799   work   n. (ii)

employment   job   livelihood

calling   strong inner urge to follow an occupation

career   way of making a living, especially one with opportunities for advancement or promotion

craft   occupation in which skill, especially of the hands, is needed

profession   occupation requiring special training and qualifications

800   write   v.

correspond   write letters to each other regularly

draft   make a rough, preliminary written version

draw up   decide and write down something

engrave   cut or carve into a hard surface

inscribe   write or cut words on a surface

note   keep a brief record of something

record   set down in writing or other permanent form

scrawl   write in a careless, irregular, or unskilful way

scribble   write hurriedly or carelessly

transcribe   write, type, or print out fully from speech or notes

list

801   writing   n.

calligraphy   the art of producing beautiful handwriting

longhand   ordinary writing, contrasted with shorthand, typing, or printing

penmanship   skill in writing by hand

script   writing done by hand, especially with the letters of words joined

802   yellow   adj.

amber   buff   butter   daffodil
flaxen   gilt   gold   golden   honey
jaundiced   lemon   primrose   saffron
sallow   sandy   tawny

803   young   adj.

youthful

adolescent   between being a child and an adult

childish   acting like a child; unsuitable for a grown person

immature   not fully formed or developed

infantile   acting like a small child
juvenile   of or for young people
puerile   childish; silly
teenage   between 13 and 19 years of
  age

boyish   girlish   kittenish
puppy-like

804   zoo   n.

aquarium   glass container for fish and
  other water animals and plants
aviary   large cage or building for
  keeping birds
bird sanctuary   an area where birds
  are protected and encouraged to
  breed
game park   enclosed area of
  grassland, usually with trees, where
  wild animals can be viewed
menagerie   collection of wild or
  strange animals in captivity, for
  exhibition
nature reserve   large enclosed area of
  land where plants and all other forms
  of wild life are protected
safari park   park in which wild
  animals are kept so that one can
  drive round in a car and look at them
vivarium   place where live animals
  are kept under natural conditions for
  study and research

Index

If the same word appears more than once in the index the headword under which it appears is also given. The headword is also given if the entry has been divided into two parts. The headwords are printed in **bold** type.

aim   33
aim   (**end**, n.ii)   262
aim at   406
aimless   589
air   687
airless   178
alacrity   696
alarm   642
alarmed   27
album   116
ale   83
alert   34
alert, be   95
alien   714
alive   35
alive to   68
all   36
all but   (**almost**)   38
all but   (**nearly**)   503
allege   (**accuse**)   15
allege   (**say**)   640
allegory   713
all-embracing   793
all in   748
allocate   343
allot   343
allow   (**agree**)   31
allow   37
allow   (**let**, v.i)   437
allowable   535
allow to pass   437
all right   12
all the same   382
allure   65
alluring   (**charming**)   156
alluring   (**lovely**)   459
ally   330
almost   38
almost   (**nearly**)   503
alms   340
alone   451
alongside   91
aloof   759
alp   488
also   39
also   (**besides**)   93
also   (**too**   adv.i)   749
alter   152

although   40
altogether   41
always   42
amass   (**collect**)   184
amass   (**increase**)   393
amaze   223
amazing   (**fabulous**)   283
amazing   (**wonderful**)   796
amber   802
amble   778
ambition   33
amend   620
amiable   (**cheerful**)   162
amiable   (**nice**)   508
amid   43
among   43
amongst   43
amount   44
ample   (**enough**)   267
ample   (**much**)   489
amplify   393
amusement   333
amusing   (**enjoyable**)   266
amusing   (**funny**)   334
amusing   (**nice**)   508
anaemic   529
analyse   (**examine**)   273
analyse   (**think**)   742
ancestor   531
anecdote   713
anew   29
anger   734
angle   45
angle   (**subject**)   716
angry   46
angry   (**mad**)   462
anguish   528
animal   47
animate   402
animated   (**bright**)   126
animated   (**lively**)   449
animosity   698
annotate   512
announce   (**reveal**)   618
announce   (**say**)   640
annoy   730
annoyed   45
annoying   48

annual 324
annul 3
anorak 180
another 49
another time 29
anonymous 496
answer v.(i) 50
answer v.(ii) 51
antagonism 698
antagonist 263
antagonistic 614
anthem 687
anthology 116
anticipate (**expect**) 279
anticipate (**look for**, v.ii) 455
antiquated 516
anxiety 139
anyhow adv.(i) 52
anyhow adv.(ii) 53
anyway 52
apart from (**besides**) 93
apart from (**except**) 275
apartment 379
apathetic 536
apex 750
aphorism 573
apiece 250
apologize 604
appalling 307
apparatus 741
apparently (**probably**) 566
appealing (**charming**) 156
appealing (**pretty**) 559
appear v.(i) 54
appear v.(ii) 55
appetizing 238
applaud (**cheer**, v.i) 161
application 257
appoint 495
appointment 415
appreciate (**know**, v.i) 427
apprehend (**grasp**, v.ii) 352
apprehend (**understand**) 761
apprehension 139
apprehensive 27
approach n. (**angle**) 45
approach v. 56
approach (**come**) 186
approach (**contact**) 196

approaching 6
appropriate adj. 319
appropriate v. 339
appropriate, be 32
approve 31
approved 520
approximately 6
apt 319
aptitude 2
aquarium 804
aquamarine 109
Arab 381
arbitrary 589
arbitrate 231
archipelago 409
ardently 251
area 692
argue 57
argument 629
arid 108
Armageddon 781
armchair 151
aroma 643
around 58
arrangement 549
arrant 107
arrest 146
arrival 222
arrive 186
arrive at (**reach**, v.i) 593
arrogance 561
arrogant (**boastful**) 111
arrogant (**proud**) 572
artful 59
artful (**cunning**) 214
artful (**sly**) 676
article 89
articulate 640
artless 328
as an alternative to 404
as a case in point 497
as a substitute for 404
ascend 176
as far as one can see 272
ashamed 60
ashen 357
ashen 529
asinine 666
ask 61

befriend   374
beg   61
beggarly   548
begin   85
beginning   222
begrudge   86
beguile   181
beguiling   156
behave   19
behind schedule   432
behind time   432
behold   453
beholder   694
belabour   (**emphasize**)   259
belabour   (**hit**)   377
belfry   753
belief   87
belief   (**opinion**)   524
believe   88
believe   (**think**)   742
belittling   657
bellow   663
belly   709
belongings   89
below   760
bemoan   604
bemuse   754
bench   648
bend   90
beneath   760
benefit   v.   339
benefit   n.   568
beneficial   349
bent   341
bequest   340
berate   599
bereft of   260
beret   368
beseech   61
beseige   63
beside   91
besides   adv.   92
besides   prep.   93
besmirched   103
best   318
bestow   343
bestride   668
betray   94
between   743

bewail   604
beware   95
be wary   95
bewilder   223
bewildered   (**blank**, adj.ii)   106
bewildered   (**confused**)   194
be worthy of   240
beyond   96
biased   762
bickering   580
bicycle   771
biennial   324
big   97
big-headed   572
bight   80
billowy   98
bin   (**box**)   120
bin   (**container**)   197
bind   745
binoculars   731
biography   713
bird sanctuary   804
birth   222
bit   99
biting   100
bitter   n.   83
bitter   adj.(i)   100
bitter   adj.(ii)   101
bitter   adj.(iii)   102
bitter   (**cold**)   183
bizarre   518
blab   618
black   103
blacklist   79
blackmailer   739
blame   104
blanch   286
blanched   529
blank   adj.(i)   105
blank   adj.(ii)   106
blare   690
blasé   141
blasphemous   498
blast   690
blatant   107
blaze   n.   317
blaze   v.   658
blazer   180
bleach   286

by the way   392

cabinet   120
cable   626
cackle   434
caddy   120
cadence   621
cagey   676
cajole   181
calamitous   306
calamity   13
calculating   59
call   495
calligraphy   801
calling   799
callous   130
call out   663
calm   adj.(i)   136
calm   adj.(ii)   137
camouflage   375
campaign   781
candid   328
cannon   360
canny   59
canoe   112
cap   368
capability   2
capable   256
capaciousness   692
capacity   (**ability**)   2
capacity   (**space**)   692
cape   429
capricious   518
captivate   735
captivating   (**charming**)   156
captivating   (**pretty**)   559
captive   562
capture   v.   146
car   138
car   (**vehicle**)   771
carbine   360
carbon   203
cardinal   601
care   139
career   799
care for   458
careful   140
careful, be   95

careless   141
careless   (**remiss**)   610
carelessly   53
caress   751
careworn   142
cargo   450
carmine   601
carouse   246
carp   493
carpet bag   75
carriage   771
carrier   75
carry   143
cart   v.   143
cart   n.   771
carton   120
carve   215
cascade   v.   323
cascade   n.   623
case   144
casket   120
cast   744
cast around for   454
cast aspersions on   104
castigate   644
cast-offs   420
casual   adj.(i)&(ii)   145
casual   (**random**)   589
casually   392
catalogue   n.   446
catalogue   v.   512
catapult   744
cataract   623
catastrophe   13
catastrophic   306
cat-burglar   739
catcall   663
catch   146
catching   147
catchphrase   673
category   170
cater   721
catnap   672
cause   v.   128
cause   n.   148
caustic   102
cautious   140
cavalcade   567
cavil   57

cease 710
celebrate 149
celebrated 150
celebrity 293
cement 303
censure 192
cerise 601
certainly (**absolutely**) 8
certainly (**truly**) 755
certainty 87
certificate 530
certified 520
chafe 630
chagrined 60
chain v. 416
chain n. 488
chair 151
chair (**seat**) 648
chalice 346
chalky 792
challenge 236
champion 295
chance (**accidental**) 14
chance (**happen**) 364
chance (**random**) 589
chance upon (**find**) 314
chance upon (**meet**) 476
change v. (**affect**, v.i) 25
change v. 152
changeable 153
change into 81
chant v. 667
chant n. 687
chaos 154
chaotic 480
character 155
character (**nature**) 500
characterize 235
characteristic 397
charge 560
charitable 508
charm 65
charming 156
charming (**lovely**) 459
chart 469
charter v. 438
charter n. 530
chary 140
chase 157

chaste 575
chastise 644
chat 725
chattels 350
chatter (**shake**) 656
chatter (**talk**) 725
cheap 158
cheat 159
check 711
cheek 160
cheer 161
cheerful (**bright**, adj.ii) 126
cheerful 162
cheerfully 345
cheering 163
cheering (**nice**) 508
cheerless (**bleak**) 108
cheerless 164
cheery 162
cheese-paring 483
chequered 153
cherish 458
cherry 601
chest 120
chestnut 417
chew 253
chide (**rebuke**) 599
chide (**scold**) 644
chief 464
chiefly 165
chiefly (**mainly**) 465
child (**boy**) 121
child (**girl**) 342
childish (**silly**) 666
childish (**young**) 803
chilly 183
chime 690
china 210
chip 123
chirp 667
chivalrous 122
chock-a-block 332
choke 166
choose 167
chop 786
chore 415
chortle 434
christen 495
chronic 168

echo 611
economical 158
economize 639
edge 254
edgy 616
edit 620
educate 728
education 428
educationalist 729
effect 255
effective (**telling**) 733
effective (**useful**) 767
effectiveness 264
effects (**belongings**) 89
efficient 256
effort 257
effortlessly 252
ego 155
egotistic 653
elated 344
elbow 410
elbow grease 264
elect 167
elegant 559
element 532
elephantine 97
elevate 441
elsewhere 258
elucidate 235
elude 268
emaciated 740
embankment 779
embark (**begin**) 85
embark (**go**) 347
embarrassed 60
embellishment 232
embezzle 625
embittered 614
emend 620
emerge 54
emergence 222
eminence (**fame**) 293
eminence (**hill**) 376
eminent 150
emotion 310
empower 437
emphasize 259
emphasize (**insist**) 401
employ 766

employment (**job**) 415
employment (**work**) 799
empty 260
enamour 65
enchant 65
enchanting (**charming**) 156
enchanting (**lovely**) 459
enchanting (**pretty**) 559
encounter 476
encouraging 163
encyclopaedia 116
end n.(i) 261
end n.(ii) 262
end v. (**finish**) 316
end v. (**stop**) 710
endeavour n. 33
endeavour v. 756
endlessly 42
endowment (**ability**) 2
endowment (**gift, n.i**) 340
endurance 538
endure 703
enduring 430
enemy 263
energetic 35
energize 602
energy 264
engaged 133
engaging (**charming**) 156
engaging (**pretty**) 559
engine 265
engrave 800
engraving 546
engrossing 407
enigma 578
enjoin 23
enjoy 442
enjoyable 266
enjoyable (**nice**) 508
enjoyable (**pleasant**) 550
enjoyment (**fun**) 333
enjoyment (**pleasure**) 551
enlarge 393
enlarged 724
enlightened 795
enlist 543
enormous 97
enough 267
enquire 61

ferry 659
fester 627
festival 378
fetch 339
fête 378
fetid 678
feud 580
few 311
fez 368
fib (**lie**, v.ii) 440
fibber 439
fickle 153
fiction 713
fictitious 292
fidgety 616
field-day 378
field-glasses 731
fierce 312
fiendish 637
fierce 637
fiery 601
fight 313
file 567
filled 332
filthy (**messy**) 480
filthy (**vulgar**) 775
finale 261
finally 431
find 314
fine 315
finger 751
finicky 140
finish n. 261
finish v. 316
finish v. (**stop**) 710
fiord 80
fire 317
firearm 360
firm 683
first 318
first and foremost 165
first-class (**fine**) 315
first-class (**terrific**) 736
first rate 315
fit 32
fitting (**acceptable**) 12
fitting 319
fix up 478
flabby (**fat**) 304

flabby (**soft**) 682
flaccid 682
flag v. 247
flag n. 320
flagrant 107
flair 341
flapping 325
flare 658
flare up 725
flash 658
flat adj. (**even**) 270
flat adj. 321
flat n. 379
flatter (**coax**) 181
flatter 322
flaunting 107
flaxen 802
flay 377
flee 268
fleece v. 159
fleece n. 362
fleet of foot 584
flex 90
flick 377
flicker 658
flimsy 787
flinch 208
fling 744
flinty 707
floating 325
flock together 184
flog 377
flood 323
floret 324
florid 601
flourishing 717
flout 236
flow v. 323
flow n. 621
flower 324
flurry 335
flush 622
fluster 335
fluttering 325
fly in the face of 236
flying 325
foe 263
fog 484
foil v. 711

from then on   737
frontier   119
fronting   16
frown   331
frowsy   480
frugal   483
fruitless   768
frumpy   480
fulfil   (**finish**)   316
fulfil   (**keep**)   422
fulfilment   551
full   332
full-blown   471
full-grown   (**mature**)   471
full-grown   (**adult**)   22
full of life   449
fully   (**absolutely**)   8
fully   (**quite**, adv.i)   586
fully developed   (**adult**)   22
fully developed   (**mature**)   471
fulminate   725
fuming   462
fun   333
functional   767
funereal   219
funny   334
fur   362
furious   462
furnish   721
furnished   595
further   117
further on   96
furtive   704
fuss   335
futile   768

gadget   741
gaffe   485
gag   417
gaiety   333
gain   v.   339
gain   n.   568
gala   378
gale   794
gallant   122
galleon   112
galley   112
game   336

game park   804
gang   211
gangling   740
gaol   412
gape   702
garbage   420
gargantuan   97
garner   184
garrotte   166
gash   215
gasp   337
gather   184
gathering   477
gaunt   740
gawky   72
gay   126
gaze   785
gazeteer   469
gear   89
general practitioner   244
generally   522
generator   265
generously   329
generous   508
genius   341
genre   424
gentle   338
genuine   596
genuinely   (**really**)   597
genuinely   (**truly**)   755
genus   424
get   (**accept**)   11
get   339
get away   268
get back at   50
get in touch with   196
get rid of   1
get the better of   233
get the picture   761
get through   316
get-together   477
ghastly   (**fearful**)   307
ghastly   (**pale**)   529
ghostly   529
gibberish   511
giddy   288
gift   (**ability**)   2
gift   n.(i)   340
gift   n.(ii)   341

great   463
great deal, a   489
greatcoat   180
greedy   adj.(i) & (ii)   356
green   353
green-eyed   414
grey   357
grid   469
grief   139
grieve   604
grievous   101
grim   355
grimace   (**frown**)   331
grimace   (**smile**)   679
grimy   103
grin   679
grind   v.   (**break**)   123
grind   n.   (**effort**)   257
grind   n.   (**work**, n.i)   798
grip   n.   75
grip   v.   351
gripping   708
grisly   758
groan   690
groove   361
gross   304
grotesque   (**odd**)   518
ground   429
ground swell   786
group   (**class**)   170
group   (**crowd**)   211
grouping   526
grove   797
grovel   208
grow dull   286
grow into   81
grown-up   22
grudging   474
gruesome   758
gruffly   (**shortly**, adv.ii)   662
grumble   493
guard   358
guard against   95
guarded   633
guardian   531
guerrilla warfare   781
guess   359
guffaw   434
guide   23

guideline   182
guileful   214
guileless   328
gulf   80
gulp   (**drink**)   246
gulp   (**gasp**)   337
gulp down   253
gun   360
gunmetal-grey   357
guru   729
gush   (**flow**)   323
gush   (**talk**)   725
gust   794
gut   241
guts   709
guy   626
guzzle   246
gyrate   757

habit   361
habit   (**practice**)   556
habitable   448
habitation   379
habitual   (**regular**)   605
habitual   (**usual**)   769
habitually   522
hacienda   300
haggard   (**careworn**)   142
haggard   (**thin**)   740
hair   362
half-baked   216
half-starved   740
halyard   626
hammock   82
hamper   n.   197
hamper   v.   711
handbag   75
handbook   116
handiness   671
handiwork   798
handle   751
handout   115
handsome   559
handy   201
hang   363
hang   (**kill**)   423
hanging   325
haphazard   (**accidental**)   14

irritable   46
irritated   462
irritating   48
island   409
isle   409
islet   409
issue   (**effect**)   255
issue   (**question**)   583
isthmus   429
itchy   616
item   285
ivory   792

jab   410
jabber   725
jacket   180
jack-knife   426
jackpot   564
jagged   411
jail   412
jailbird   562
jalopy   138
jamboree   378
jammed   746
jam-packed   332
jangle   509
jar   197
jaundiced   802
jaunt   418
jaunty   413
jealous   414
jealous of, be   86
jealousy   698
jeep   (**car**)   138
jeep   (**vehicle**)   771
jeering   636
jelly-like   682
jeopardy   218
jerkin   180
jest   417
jet   323
jettison   1
jingle   509
jitters   642
jittery   27
job   415
job   (**work**)   799
jocular   334

jog   576
join   416
joke   417
joking   333
jollity   333
jolly   413
jolt   576
jostle   576
journal   116
journey   418
jovial   162
joyful   162
judge   (**assess**)   62
judge   (**compare**)   189
judgement   524
judicious   795
jumble   179
jumbled   490
jump   419
jumpy   616
juncture   747
junk   420
just   (**fair**)   289
just   421
just   (**merely**)   479
just about   (**almost**)   38
just about   (**nearly**)   503
justify   51
juvenile   (**boy**)   121
juvenile   (**girl**)   342
juvenile   (**young**)   803

kayak   112
keenly   251
keep   422
keep safe   358
keyed up   616
kill   423
kill time   776
kin   424
kind   n.   424
kindly   508
king   425
kinsmen   540
kit   89
kitbag   75
kittenish   803
knack   671

knead 630
knell 690
knife 426
knock 377
knock back 246
knock off (**kill**) 423
knock off (**rob**) 625
knoll 376
know v.(i) & (ii) 427
know-how 671
knowing 59
knowledge 428
knowledgeable 557

labour 798
lacerate 171
lack 780
lad 121
lag 237
lager 83
lagging 674
laid up 387
lament 604
lamentable 537
land 429
landscape 773
languish 247
lanky 740
lapis lazuli 109
large 97
large quantity 457
lash 745
lass 342
lassie 342
lasting 430
lastly 431
late (**former**) 326
late 432
late (**sometime**) 684
lately 433
later 28
latest 764
laugh 434
laughable 666
launch v. 85
launch n. 112
launder 783
laundered 172

lavish 622
law 182
lawful 520
lawn 353
lax 398
lay 577
lay down 235
lay out 697
laze (**lie**, v.i) 440
lazy 435
lead 128
leaden 357
leading question 583
leak 618
lean 740
leap 419
leapfrog 419
learning 428
lease 438
leathery 752
leave 1
leave-taking 534
leavings 420
lecture (**rebuke**) 599
lecture (**talk**) 725
lecturer 729
ledger 116
leer 453
leeway 692
left-overs 420
legal 520
legend 713
legitimate 520
legwork 798
leisurely 674
lemon 802
lend 438
lend a hand 374
lenient 398
lest 436
let (**allow**) 37
let v.(i) 437
let v.(ii) 438
lethal 305
lethargic 435
level (**even**) 270
level (**flat**) 321
lever 441
levy 560

lewd   775
liable to   595
liar   439
libeller   439
liberate   613
licence   530
licensed   520
lie   v.(i) & (ii)   440
lifeless   225
lift   441
light-footed   30
light-hearted   162
light upon   314
light-weight   447
like   442
likeable   508
likely   443
likely   566
liken   189
likeness   (**copy**)   203
likeness   444
liking   445
lilt   621
limit   (**boundary**)   119
limit   (**edge**)   254
limp   adj.   682
limp   v.   778
limousine   138
limpid   173
lineaments   284
liner   659
line-up   446
linger   237
link   416
liquidate   423
list   n.   446
list   v.   800
literal   204
litter   179
little   447
little   (**small**)   677
liveable   448
livelihood   (**job**)   415
livelihood   (**work**, n.ii)   799
lively   (**bright**)   126
lively   449
load   (**heap**)   371
load   450
load   (**lot**)   457

loaded question   583
loathe   v.   369
loathing   198
loathsome   (**rotten**, adj.i)   628
locale   603
locate   (**find**)   314
locate   (**put**)   577
lock   78
locker   120
lock up   v.   78
lock-up   n.   412
lodge   703
lodgings   379
log   116
logical   598
loiter   776
loll   (**lie**, v.i)   440
lonely   adj.(i)   451
lonely   adj.(ii)   452
long for   780
longhand   801
long-lived   430
long-standing   168
look   453
look as if   55
look black   331
look daggers   331
look for   v.(i)   454
look for   v.(ii)   455
look for   (**seek**)   651
look like   55
look up   196
look up to   21
loom   54
loop   90
loose   (**baggy**)   76
loose   456
loot   565
lorry   771
lorryload   450
lot   (**amount**)   44
lot   457
lottery   564
lounge   668
loutish   631
love   458
lovely   459
lovely   (**pretty**)   559
lowly   475

munch 253
murder 423
murderous 312
murky 164
muscle-bound 715
muse 742
musket 360
must 492
mustang 381
muster 184
musty 701
muted (**inaudible**) 391
muted (**quiet**) 585
mutilated 758
mutter 725
mystery 578
mystified (**confused**) 194
myth 713

nab 351
nag n. 381
nag v. 493
nagging 48
naked 494
name 495
name (**reputation**) 612
nameless 496
namely 497
nap 672
narrate 732
narration 713
narrow-minded 474
nasty (**awful**, adj.ii) 70
nasty adj.(i) 498
nasty adj.(ii) 499
nation 540
native land 429
naturally 329
nature (**character**) 155
nature 500
nature reserve 804
naughty (adj.i) 501
naughty (adj.ii) 502
nauseating (**smelly**) 678
nauseating (**ugly**) 758
nearby 201
nearly (**almost**) 38
nearly 503

near to 91
necessary 269
need 780
needy 554
neglect (**ignore**) 386
neglect 504
neglectful (**careless**) 141
neglectful (**remiss**) 610
negligent (**careless**) 141
negligent (**remiss**) 610
negligently 53
never-ending 430
nervous 27
net 146
nettled (**angry**) 46
nettled (**mad**) 462
neutral 421
nevertheless (**but**) 135
nevertheless (**however**) 382
nevertheless 505
newborn 73
newsmonger 134
newspaper 506
newsprint 530
next adj.(i) & (ii) 507
next (**then**) 737
next to 91
nibble 253
nice 508
nick 625
nick-nack 232
niggardly 483
nimble 30
noble (**good**, adj.i) 348
noble (**magnificent**) 463
nod off 672
noise 509
noisome 678
nominate 495
nonchalant (**casual**, adj.i) 145
none 510
none the less 505
non-participating 536
nonplus 223
non-plussed 194
non-plussed 695
nonsense 511
nonsensical 666
no-one 510

pose 577
position 577
positively 597
possess 370
possessions 89
possessive 414
possible 555
possibly (**maybe**) 472
possibly (**perhaps**) 542
post 654
postpone (**delay**) 237
postpone (**wait**) 776
postulate 88
pot-bellied 304
pot-belly 709
potentate 425
potential 2
pother 335
pottery 210
pouch 75
pounce 419
poverty-stricken 554
power 2
powerful 715
practicable 555
practical 767
practice (**habit**) 361
practice 556
practised (**experienced**) 280
practised 557
pragmatic 598
prairie 354
praise 322
prattle 725
preach 725
precedent 274
precipice 488
precise 204
precipitate 591
precipitately 367
precipitous 705
precocious 175
predicament 552
predict 558
predominant 464
predominantly 165
pre-eminent 693
prefer 167
preferably 404

preference 445
prejudiced 762
preliminary 670
premonition 310
preoccupied 759
preparatory 670
prepared (**alert**) 34
prepared (**ready**) 595
prepared to 5
preposterous 666
prescribe 23
present n. (**bonus**) 115
present n. (**gift**, n.i) 340
present v. (**give**) 343
present v. (**show**) 664
presentable 535
presentiment 310
present-day (**up-to-date**) 764
present-day (**modern**) 486
presently 688
preserve (**keep**) 422
press 751
press forward 576
pressing 765
prestige 293
presume 722
presumption 561
pretend 19
pretty (**lovely**) 459
pretty 559
prevailing 527
prevail upon 543
prevaricator 439
prevent 711
previous 326
previously 84
price 560
pride 561
primarily 465
primary 318
primed 595
primitive 637
primrose 802
principal 318
principally (**chiefly**) 165
principally (**mainly**) 465
principles 182
prison 412
prisoner 562

purpose (**end**, n.ii) 262
purposeless 553
purse 75
pursue 157
push 576
put 577
put away 246
put back together 478
put down 581
put forward 719
put off 237
putrefy 627
putrid (**rotten**, adj.ii) 628
putrid (**smelly**) 678
put right 478
put up 131
put up with 37
puzzle 578
pyramid 753

quaff 246
quagmire 113
quail 208
quaint 714
quake 656
qualified 280
qualified for, be 240
qualm 579
quandary 552
quantity 44
quarrel 580
quarrel (**row**) 629
queer 518
quell 581
quench 582
query v. 61
query n. 583
quest 418
question (**ask**) 61
question 583
quibble 57
quick (**fast**) 302
quick 584
quick-witted 615
quiet (**calm**, adj.i) 136
quiet 585
quill 308
quip 417

quit 710
quite adv.(i) & (ii) 586
quiver 656
quiz 61
quotation 560

rabble (**crowd**) 211
rabble 587
race (**people**) 540
racket 509
radiant 125
radiate 658
radio 654
rage 725
ragged 411
raging (**angry**) 46
raging (**mad**) 462
ragtag and bobtail 587
raid 63
rail against 10
rain 588
raincoat 180
raise 441
raise aloft 441
raise high 441
ramble (**talk**) 725
ramble (**walk**) 778
rampart 779
ranch 300
rancid 691
random 589
range 488
rank adj.(i) & (ii) 590
rank (**smelly**) 678
ransack 651
ransom 613
rant 725
ranting 46
rap 377
rapacious (**greedy**, adj.i) 356
rapid 302
rapidity 696
rapids 623
rapier 426
rare 693
rarely 652
rash 591
rasp v. 630

unstable 153
unstained 172
unsuitable 71
unsure 763
unsympathetic (**heartless**) 372
untamed 637
untidy 480
untied 456
untimely 71
untouched 405
untrue 292
untrustworthy 205
unusual (**odd**) 518
unusual (**strange**) 714
unvaried (**boring**) 118
unvaried (**even**) 270
unveil 664
unwanted 451
unwary 591
unwell 387
unwieldy (**awkward**, adj.i) 71
unwieldy (**weighty**, adj.i) 789
unwise 666
unworried 759
unyielding 707
upbraid (**rebuke**) 599
upbraid (**scold**) 644
update 620
upheaval 154
uphold 441
uplift 402
upright 421
uproar 509
upset 154
upshot 255
up-to-date (**modern**) 486
up-to-date 764
urchin 121
urge 23
urgent 765
usable 767
usage 361
use 766
useful (**convenient**) 201
useful 767
usefulness 770
useless 768
usual (**regular**) 605
usual 769

usually 522
utilize 766
utter 640
utterly 8

vacant 260
vacation 378
vague 287
vain 553
valiant 122
valid 596
validation 570
valuation 560
value 770
vandalize 699
vanity 561
vanquish (**defeat**) 233
vanquish (**quell**) 581
vapour 484
variable 153
variety 424
various 468
vast 97
vastness 692
vault 419
vaunting 111
veer 245
vehemently 251
vehicle 771
veil 375
veld 354
velocity 696
venal (**greedy**, adj.i) 356
vendetta 580
venerable 150
venerate 21
venom 698
venomous 305
ventilate 618
venture 756
verge 254
verify 193
versed 557
very (**so**, adj.i) 681
very 772
vessel (**container**) 197
vessel (**ship**) 659
vex 730

well-coordinated   30
well-founded   598
well-grounded   280
well-heeled   622
well-known   294
wellnigh   38
well-pleased   344
well-provided   595
well-to-do   622
wench   342
wet   791
whaler   659
wheedle   181
wheel   757
wheelchair   151
wheeze   124
whether   385
whimper   213
whimsical   296
whimsy   417
whine   213
whisper   640
white   792
whole-hearted   373
wholesale price   560
wholesale store   660
wholesome   575
wholly   (**absolutely**)   8
wholly   (**altogether**)   41
whoop   663
wicked   74
wide   793
wide-awake   (**alert**)   34
wide-awake   (**wakeful**)   777
wide-ranging   793
widespread   793
wield   766
wild   312
will   530
willingly   345
wile   181
wilt   247
wilted   701
wily   (**cunning**)   214
wily   (**sly**)   676
wind   794
windcheater   180
windfall   564
winding-up   261

windswept   108
wineglass   346
winning   156
winnings   564
win over   543
winsome   (**charming**)   156
winsome   (**pretty**)   559
wipe out   241
wiry   740
wise   795
wisecrack   417
wish for   780
withdrawn   665
withered   701
with good grace   345
withhold   639
within   390
within reach   201
without a stitch on   494
without end   42
with pleasure   345
with reference to   191
witness   785
witticism   417
wizened   740
woe-begone   632
wold   354
wolf   253
wonderful   (**fabulous**)   283
wonderful   (**fantastic**)   297
wonderful   (**terrific**)   736
wonderful   796
wood   797
woodland   797
word-of-honour   774
work   (**job**)   415
work   n.(i)   798
work   n.(ii)   799
working   133
workshop   660
world-wide   793
worn-out   748
worry   139
worship   458
worth   770
worthy   12
worthy of, be   240
wound   383
wrangle   (**quarrel**)   580